CHALLENGING
MATHEMATICAL
TEASERS

CHALLENGING MATHEMATICAL TEASERS

J.A.H. HUNTER

DOVER PUBLICATIONS, INC.
NEW YORK

Published in Canada by General Publishing Company, Ltd.,
30 Lesmill Road, Don Mills, Toronto, Ontario.
Published in the United Kingdom by Constable and Company, Ltd.

Challenging Mathematical Teasers is a new work, first
published by Dover Publications, Inc., in 1980.

International Standard Book Number: 0-486-23852-0
Library of Congress Catalog Card Number: 79-51888

Manufactured in the United States of America
Dover Publications, Inc.
31 East 2nd Street
Mineola, N.Y. 11501

PREFACE

In previous collections of my problems the more difficult have been avoided. But there seems to be a growing demand for problems at a somewhat more challenging level.

The two Appendices provide brief outlines of concepts that may not be familiar to some readers, concepts that are dealt with more fully in textbooks.

Once again I must thank the thousands of kind newspaper and magazine readers whose encouragement, loyal support, and even ideas have been largely responsible for publication of this little book.

Have fun!

J. A. H. HUNTER

January 1979

CONTENTS

	TEASERS	*Problem Page*	*Solution Page*
1.	Pecking Order	1	37
2.	For the One That Got Away	1	37
3.	Long Odds	2	38
4.	Like Father Like Son	2	38
5.	Who Spilled the Coffee?	2	39
6.	So Far Apart	3	40
7.	All Twos	3	40
8.	Those Shares	3	41
9.	You Have to Know How	3	41
10.	Savings	4	41
11.	A Random Mailing	4	42
12.	No Computer for This	4	42
13.	At the Diner	5	43
14.	They Don't Come Singly	5	43
15.	Who Glubs Glygons?	5	43
16.	Three in a Row	6	44
17.	A Switch	6	44
18.	Just Triangles	6	45
19.	An Ancient Problem	7	45
20.	Similar but Different	7	46
21.	Just for Kids	7	46
22.	The Patio	7	47
23.	Squares and Squares	8	47
24.	Wrong but Right	8	48

		Problem Page	Solution Page
25.	The Stamp	8	48
26.	A Tale of Two Guys	9	49
27.	Just Junk	9	49
28.	A Simple Routine	9	49
29.	Commemoration Stamps	10	50
30.	Almost Neighbors	10	50
31.	Real Estate	11	51
32.	Greetings	11	51
33.	Away from It All	11	52
34.	Double the Odds	12	52
35.	Bounty Hunters	12	53
36.	The Mural	13	53
37.	A Woman's Job	13	54
38.	Each to Each	13	54
39.	The Jewel Box	14	55
40.	Peter's Pennies	14	55
41.	So Very Simple	15	56
42.	Power Play	15	56
43.	The Collector	15	56
44.	A Matter of Squares	16	57
45.	The Only Tree	16	57
46.	It Makes Sense	16	58
47.	Grandad's Birthday	17	59
48.	Vandalism	17	59
49.	Transportation	17	59
50.	Just for Fun	18	60
51.	Good Service	18	60
52.	Both Hands	18	61
53.	Long Odds	19	61
54.	The Talkative Guest	19	62
55.	Uranium Triangles	19	62
56.	Men on the Moon	20	63
57.	A Friendly Teller	20	63
58.	Many a Mickle	20	64
59.	A Tale of Woe	21	64
60.	Quite a Family	21	65
61.	Numbers, Numbers	22	65
62.	The Years That Count	22	66
63.	A Funny Fraction	22	66
64.	Two Magic Squares	22	66

		Problem Page	Solution Page
65.	The Joker's Wild	23	67
66.	Easy Come Easy Go	23	67
67.	A Bug in a Barn	24	68
68.	Wrong Number	24	68
69.	At the Show	24	69
70.	The Penalty Clause	25	69
71.	Consecutive Squares	25	70
72.	Think of a Number	25	70
73.	A Deal in Stamps	26	71
74.	A Serial Number	26	71
75.	An Evening Out	27	71
76.	A Matter of Ages	27	72
77.	Dropping in on Len	27	72
78.	Cards on the Table	28	73
79.	A Bus Ride	28	73
80.	You're Sure If in Doubt	29	74
81.	Creepy Crawlies	29	74
82.	Family Numbers	29	75
83.	Too Many Girls	30	75
84.	What? No Zobblies?	30	76
85.	The Census	30	76
86.	A Whiz Kid	31	76
87.	Tickets in the Sweep	31	77
88.	Progress	31	77
89.	Three Times	32	78
90.	A Touching Tale	32	78
91.	Fun for Some	32	79
92.	He Broke the Bank	33	79
93.	Do It Yourself	33	80
94.	A Bug for the Birds	33	81
95.	A Lucky Number	34	81
96.	A Matter of Time	34	82
97.	The Poster	34	83
98.	At the Casino	35	83
99.	No Direct Road	35	84
100.	A Nest Egg	35	84
	ALPHAMETICS	87	93
	APPENDICES	97	

CHALLENGING
MATHEMATICAL
TEASERS

TEASERS

1. PECKING ORDER

Four sparrows found a dish of seed,
Fine birdie food, no common weed.
Said Pip: "In turn each take two grains
And then a third of what remains.
It's me as first, then Pep, then Pop,
With Pap the last. And then we stop."

But Pap cried out: "It isn't fair.
Mine's two seeds less than half Pep's share."
Old Pip was boss, his word was law,
So little Pap got nothing more.
Poor Pap, his share was rather small!
How many seeds were there in all?

2. FOR THE ONE THAT GOT AWAY

Steve was picking out some trout flies from a box on the counter. "Do you have those new lures you told me about?" he asked. "They sounded interesting."

"All gone. I only got in a few to see how they'd sell, and I've ordered more," Clem replied. "I sold the lot at as many cents each as the square of the number I had."

Steve smiled. "I'll take your word for that, but I would like a few when you have them."

"Okay, and you can figure out the price yourself," Clem told him. "All the same as before, and my percentage markup was what I had to pay in cents per lure."

What was his selling price?

3. LONG ODDS

Charlie stopped at the table. He drew four cards from the little heap there, and turned them up. "Look, Pam!" he exclaimed. "The four aces."

His wife smiled. "You don't have a complete deck there. The kids were playing and some cards are missing," she told him. "But you wouldn't do that again in a thousand years."

"Want to bet?" Charlie had checked the deck and done some quick figuring. "In fact the odds were exactly a thousand to one against picking all the aces from the cards that were there."

How many cards were there?

4. LIKE FATHER LIKE SON

Sam smiled. "You're a puzzle fan, so what about this?" he asked. "If you take your age from the square of the sum of its digits you get Ann's age. And the same goes for my age."

"That's great, Dad, and you're right," replied Mike, checking on a scrap of paper. "But you need something else. The square of the sum of the four digits in your age and mine is just one less than twice the total of our two ages."

Well, how old was Ann?

5. WHO SPILLED THE COFFEE?

Harry had an invoice in his hand. "Look at this," he said. "Someone has spilled coffee on it, and now I can't make out the total amount."

Susan looked. "That's too bad, but it wasn't me," she told him. "It's for one lot of knives at $2.96 each, but the number invoiced is unreadable."

"The total is not completely obliterated." Harry pointed to the entry. "It was for a 4-figure number of dollars and some cents. Only the first figure of the dollars and the last of the cents are illegible. You can still see 704 of the dollars, and a 9 as the first figure of the cents. We can figure it out."

You try.

6. SO FAR APART

It was a cold, wet Sunday afternoon, and of course there was nothing worth watching on TV. But Ted seemed quite happy at the old desk in the corner.

Suddenly he put down his pen. "I've figured out something with our phone number and Sonia's," he said.

"The girl you met in Austria?" Jeff asked. "Okay let's have it."

Ted grinned. "It's only math. Seven times the cube of her 7-digit number is exactly three times the seventh power of the 4-figure part of ours."

He was right, so what were the numbers?

7. ALL TWOS

Jane held up a couple of invoices. "Look at these totals, both for $222.22. Three items in each, and all at different prices."

Harry looked. "That's a coincidence," he commented.

"But there's more to it than that. For each of the six items the dollar amount is the square of what's in the cents column."

What were the amounts?

8. THOSE SHARES

"I did agree to be Elmer's executor," said Don, "but I never realized what an oddball the old chap was."

Clare smiled. "He was a dear, and anyway you only have to see that his wishes are carried out."

"Only!" Her husband chuckled. "Here's just one item in his will. He left his 409 Cosmos shares to his three sons, on the condition that the square of the number of one son's shares be equal to the product of the other two. And I can't figure it out."

There was nothing wrong with Elmer's arithmetic, so how would those shares be apportioned?

9. YOU HAVE TO KNOW HOW

"Try multiplying your age by seven, Dad," said Len. "The quick way."

Tom smiled. "There's only one way I know, but I'm not sure I can do it in my head."

"Sure you can," Len told him. "Just take the digits in the opposite order and put the proper digit between them."

The boy was right. So how old was Tom, and what was that special digit?

10. SAVINGS

"So you let Stan empty his money box. I guess he'd lost interest anyway," said Sally. "Was there much in it?"

"Not much, but it's funny the way it was," her husband replied. "The dimes, nickels and quarters were all prime numbers, all different. And there were as many pennies as the number of dimes multiplied by the total of dimes and nickels."

"What about the quarters?" Sally asked.

Mike smiled. "A good question, but figure it out for yourself. There were twenty-four more pennies than quarters, and that's all the money there was."

How much did the box contain?

11. A RANDOM MAILING

"A little job for you," said Sam, handing George a card index box. "Pick at random and mail our new folders to a fair sampling of these people. About five percent, say."

But George had a plan. He would pick the first, miss one, pick the next, miss two, pick the next, miss three, and so on.

And his scheme worked, for his final card was actually the last card of the index. Furthermore, when he checked he found he had picked exactly five percent of the total number.

How many had he picked?

12. NO COMPUTER FOR THIS

Ron had been busy at the table quite awhile. "I give up!" he exclaimed suddenly, throwing down his pen. "You'd need a computer."

"Come on, it can't be that tough," his father told him. "But what's the problem?"

"Something our math teacher gave us," the boy replied. "We have to find an 8-figure number that is one-third what you get when you add the square of its first four digits to the square of the last four."

Certainly a tough problem, but it could be solved without too much numerical working. Try it!

13. AT THE DINER

The place was crowded, and they were lucky to get a table to themselves. Now they sat there impatiently, six hungry young people, waiting for their food.

Ron sat on the left of the girl who sat on the left of the man who sat on Joan's left, and Ann sat on the left of the man who sat on the left of the girl who sat on the left of the man who sat on the left of the girl who sat on the left of Pam's husband, while Steve sat on the right of the girl who sat on Harry's right.

Pam was not next to her husband, but which of the three men was he?

14. THEY DON'T COME SINGLY

Fred put down his pen. "No wonder my total was $13.33 wrong," he said. "I entered the dollars as cents and the cents as dollars for Bradley's check."

Helen smiled. "That wasn't very smart. But I thought they paid quite a bit more."

"You're right," Fred agreed. "But it must have been my off day. I entered the same payment twice, each time making the same fool mistake."

What was the actual amount?

15. WHO GLUBS GLYGONS?

The four fallians had been gathering glygons for quite a while when Flab called a halt. "We've got nearly a thousand," he declared. "Let's share them out."

As the others watched, Flab counted out a quarter of the total for himself. "Here's one each for you to glub," he told them, flipping out three more from the heap. "Now it's Flib's turn."

Flib took a quarter of what remained, and also one each for Flob and Flub. Then Flob took a quarter of what Flib had left, and one extra glygon for Flub. And finally Flub took his quarter.

"That's fine," said Flab, one tentacle reaching into the much-depleted heap. "We can divide the rest equally among us."

How many had they gathered?

16. THREE IN A ROW

"That's interesting!" Ray leaned back in his chair. "If you write down the ages of our three kids in a row and divide that 3-digit number by the sum of their ages you get thirty-two."

Fran shook her head. "You and your figures. What's so special about that?"

"Well, it's your age, for one thing," her husband replied. "Maybe you forgot."

How old were the children?

17. A SWITCH

Martin had a piece of paper in his hand. "Here's something I just figured out about our new phone number," he said. "The complete seven figures."

"I hate it. It was so much easier to remember a word or even letters," Sally replied. "But what did you find?"

"Look," Martin told her, pointing to the paper. "If you switch the two parts, putting the four digits in front, you get one more than twice our complete number."

So what was it?

18. JUST TRIANGLES

Mike put down his ruler. "That's it. Look at the triangles I've drawn, Dad," he said. "Each area is exactly two-thirds its perimeter."

"You mean in square inches and inches?" Victor looked. "One of them seems kind of thin."

"Sure, but it is a triangle. All the sides of these triangles are whole numbers of inches."

What were the dimensions of Mike's triangles?

19. AN ANCIENT PROBLEM

Peter put down his pen. "It's just something I've figured out on ages," he said. "My age and the ages of Aunt Bessie and Uncle Joe. When you total any pair of those ages you get a perfect square."

Harry studied the sheet of paper on the table. "An odd coincidence," he told the boy. "But there's another one. Those three ages also total the square of your cousin Sally's age, and she's not yet in her teens."

What were the four ages?

20. SIMILAR BUT DIFFERENT

Doug turned when his father came into the room. "Look at the two triangles I've drawn," he said. "The sides are all exact numbers of inches."

"Using my best drawing board, eh?" Tom smiled. "But what's so special about them? I can see they're exactly similar, one bigger than the other."

"That's only part of it, Dad," the boy replied. "Exactly the same shape, but two sides of one are the same lengths as two sides of the other. And there's nineteen inches difference between the sides that are not the same."

What were the dimensions?

21. JUST FOR KIDS

Stan put down the big carton and flopped into a chair. "I left one out in the car," he said. "All crazy hats, and I hope they sell."

"Sure they will," his wife replied. "The kids ask for them all the time, the crazier the better. I hope you got a fair selection."

"As you said." Stan nodded. "Three styles, three different prices. All in even dozens, and I bought as many at each price as that price in cents. They averaged exactly half a dollar each for the lot."

How many had he bought?

22. THE PATIO

Bill was busy in his backyard when Fred arrived. "I just finished our new patio," he said. "Now it only needs some flowers in the middle."

It was a most unusual patio, but then Bill was always eccentric. He had paved three square areas, with corners meeting so that they formed the sides of an unpaved, enclosed triangle. "Fine and dandy, but it does look a bit odd," Fred commented. "Really three little patios."

"That's right," Bill agreed. "I made their areas 196, 97 and 41 square feet."

His friend smiled. "What about the flower bed in the middle?"

A good question! What was its area?

23. SQUARES AND SQUARES

Sam was busy at his desk when Joe went in, crumpled paper littering the rug around his chair.

"Trying to do Jack's homework?" Joe asked. "Kids are smart these days."

"No, it's something I made up myself, and it's a dandy," Sam replied. "If you add our house number to the product of that number and Jack's age you get twice the square of my age. But if you add Jack's age to that same product you get twice the square of my wife's age."

It was a neat little problem. What were the ages of Sam and his wife?

24. WRONG BUT RIGHT

Wendy watched with growing impatience as the clerk made out the check for her purchases. "Say!" she exclaimed at last. "You multiplied the three amounts instead of adding them. That's crazy."

"Sure I did, but it's okay," the young man replied. "The total comes to $5.70 either way. Add them up yourself."

Indeed he was right! So what were the individual amounts?

25. THE STAMP

"So that's a Kalotan stamp," Harry commented. "A great design. Do you have any more?"

"Not now. I did have a 3 kuk, a 9 kuk, a 10 kuk, a 12 kuk, a 13 kuk and a 14 kuk," Andy replied. "But at the airport I used five of them to mail a couple of postcards.

One took twice as much postage as the other, and that left me only this one stamp."

What was its value?

26. A TALE OF TWO GUYS

Mary was still busy with the dishes when Fred came in. "I guess the power's been off," he commented. "No dishwasher."

"Most of the day," replied his wife. "It only came on just now, but how did you know?"

"They were clearing up down the road around a new pole and I talked to the linesmen there," Fred told her. "It seems they fixed two guy wires on one side, both from the same band 28 feet up the pole, with their ends 150 feet apart at the ground. Their two lengths total just 250 feet, and I could see they were both taut."

Assuming the ground was level, what would the lengths of the respective guy wires be?

27. JUST JUNK

Sally flopped into her favorite chair. "I've just cleared all the junk in the attic," she said. "What a job! There was an insurance policy, but I guess it's finished."

"Probably on the old house, the one I kept because of its funny number," Greg told her. "But you got rid of those fire hazards up there, so it wouldn't matter so much anyway."

His wife smiled. "What was peculiar about the number?"

"Well, I thought it odd," Greg replied. "It had seven figures. The first, third, fifth, and last all ones. When I tried to divide it by seven, and by eleven, and by thirteen, I was one short each time. But I forget what the other three figures were."

You figure them out.

28. A SIMPLE ROUTINE

Peter put down his pen. "Dad," he said. "Did you know Uncle Fred's car plate number is like yours?"

"How's that?" John asked. "I've got a 4-figure number, but he has five figures."

The boy grinned. "I mean in one way," he explained. "You've got 6078. If you square its last three figures and then subtract the other part, you get the original number again."

His father was checking. "That's right," he declared. "The square of the last three in 6084, and subtracting 6 you get 6078. So what?"

"Well, the same routine works with Uncle Fred's number."

He was right on that too, so what was his uncle's number?

29. COMMEMORATION STAMPS

She had locked the door behind the last customer, and now Gwen was helping her husband tidy up their little store. "You know the packets of commemoration stamps we made up?" she asked. "We've got about fifty packets left. They don't sell."

"Just three different selections. Three 4¢, two 5¢ and five 10¢; seven 4¢, three 5¢ and three 10¢; one 4¢, five 5¢ and four 10¢." Paul chuckled. "I still remember that chore. Any suggestions?"

"Package those remaining stamps again but in sets of three stamps each, one stamp of each denomination," Gwen replied. "There were no spares left over, so let's check what we've got."

It didn't take long to do that, and then Paul did some figuring. "I guess you had it figured out anyway," he told her. "We're just right, not too few and not too many for your scheme."

How many stamps did they have left?

30. ALMOST NEIGHBORS

John put down the letter. "From an Elsie Brandon. She lives on your road, number 74," he said. "Maybe you know her."

"I don't recall the name, but it's a long road." Ken shook his head. "But that's funny. We have no numbers missing on the street, so there are exactly as many below her number as there are above ours."

"Then there's another coincidence." John was doing some figuring on a scrap of paper. "All the numbers above

yours, added to all below hers, total just half the total for the whole road."
What was Ken's number?

31. REAL ESTATE

"I bought that piece of land I told you about," said George. "An exact number of square yards, not far short of twelve acres. A snip for development."

"Let's hope you're right," Jack commented. "It did sound an odd shape. A sort of isosceles triangle, you told me."

His friend nodded. "Well, almost. It's a perfect triangle, but there are seven yards between the short and middle sides, and seven between the middle and the long. And it just happens that the sides are all exact numbers of yards."

Located where two highways meet, that land could have possibilities. What would its dimensions be? (Note: There are 4840 square yards in an acre.)

32. GREETINGS

Pam put down her book. "I've just realized it's Uncle Tom's birthday today," she said. "We must send the old chap a telegram."

"Okay," Doug agreed. "I'll make it out and you can phone it."

Those greetings are always difficult to word, and Doug was scribbling for quite a while. Then he looked up with a smile. "That's funny. The square of Uncle Tom's age is just one less than the difference between the cubes of Mark's and Judy's ages."

"But there's only one year between them," his wife objected. "How come?"

"The cubes of their ages," Doug replied. "You check it."
How old was Uncle Tom?

33. AWAY FROM IT ALL

"We're out in the sticks, but we do have our pick of four handy villages when the rustic scene palls," said Mike. "Maybe you saw the two roads that branch off to the northward just opposite our gates."

"Yes, I did," George replied. "Of course I came through Brill on the road that goes on to Sefton."

Mike nodded. "The other two roads go to Carlow and Lawanda, and all three are dead straight. We happen to be exactly the same distance from all four villages."

"So those are your cultural centers!" His friend smiled. "I didn't think much of Brill."

"Well, we have the choice. As the crow flies, Carlow is thirty kilometers from both Sefton and Lawanda, and Lawanda fourteen kilometers from Brill."

How far was each from Mike's gates?

34. DOUBLE THE ODDS

Jim held out a little cloth bag. "Just marbles, Dad. About forty of them, some red, the rest green," he said. "No peeking, but take one."

Don dipped into the bag and pulled out a green. Trying again he got a second green, which he placed on the table beside the first. "You can't have many reds," he commented. "What are the odds against a third green if I try once more?"

The boy thought a moment. "Just twice what they were against a red for your first draw," he replied.

How many marbles of each color did Jim have there?

35. BOUNTY HUNTERS

"Your garden was full of kids yesterday," said John. "A birthday party?"

"Sort of. Really a grub hunt combined with a party for Doug." Bob chuckled. "There were fifty kids in all."

"Smart idea," John commented. "Any prizes?"

"Sure. A quarter for every caterpillar killed. It's odd that the boys all killed the same number, and so did the girls, but not the same number as the boys," Bob replied. "But each boy had to pay me back one penny per grub for all the caterpillars the girls killed, and each girl the same for all that the boys killed. It cost me only nineteen cents per boy and eleven cents per girl, and they killed around a thousand in all."

How many girls were there?

36. THE MURAL

Steve stopped in the studio doorway. "So that's the great mural," he said. "An abstract across the complete wall. It's certainly got something, but what the heck does it mean?"

"More than you may think," Ted told him. "Tell me what you see."

His friend thought a moment. "Just lots of rectangles," he replied. "They all seem to be grouped in pairs."

Ted smiled. "That's not all. All the sides are whole numbers of inches, and in every pair the area in square inches of each equals the perimeter of the other rectangle in the pair. I drew all the pairs for which that can apply."

What were the dimensions of all his rectangles?

37. A WOMAN'S JOB

"I'll finish them." Ann went over to where her husband worked wearily, with envelopes and flyers all around him.

"Okay." Bill straightened up thankfully. "I figure I've been on the job alone for just five-twelfths as long as you'd have taken to do the lot, so maybe it's time you did some."

Ann smiled. "We've done these often enough before, so you should know," she said. "Anyway it's a woman's job."

For quite a while there was only the sound of paper sliding on paper in the little office. And then Ann stuffed the last flyer into its container. "I've been figuring too," she declared. "We would have saved just fifty-two minutes if we had worked together right through."

Bill put down his magazine, glanced at his watch, and scribbled on a scratch pad. "You're right," he told her. "And I would have done exactly half what you've actually done just now."

Next time they may have hired help. But how long had the complete job taken them?

38. EACH TO EACH

"Well, John, it's good to see you again." Bob greeted his brother. "I forgot to write thanking you all for your cards."

"Me too." John smiled. "But, talking of cards, the Doolittle family will really be boosting the card industry if we continue the way we're going. This Xmas I figure there were eighty-four more cards exchanged among all of us than the previous Xmas, and there were eighty-four more that Xmas than the one before."

Bob chuckled. "So we buy shares. It's a nice idea, though, even with all the babies included in the routine, that each member of the combined families sends a card to each other member."

How many cards had been exchanged that last Xmas?

39. THE JEWEL BOX

Jim put down the letter. "A rush order, and clear on all details except the most important one," he said. "He wants one of those square snakeskin jewel boxes, the one he says he saw here last month."

"They're all different sizes, and we're supposed to remember." Paul chuckled. "Let's ask for more information."

"He's traveling, so we can't contact him. But he wants to pick it up next week," declared his partner. "We have to set an initial in diamonds on the lid before then. Its center must be five cm from one corner of the lid, thirteen cm from the opposite corner, and eight cm from one of the corners between."

Paul thought. "Not to worry, then. There's only one of each size, and we can figure out what the size must be."

He was right, so what would be the area of the top?

40. PETER'S PENNIES

Peter had all his pennies laid out compactly on the table. "Look, Dad," he said. "They make a perfect square."

Charlie smiled. "That's right," he told the boy, breaking up the square and moving the coins into a different arrangement. "You've got just enough to make something even better. There you are, a perfect hexagon like the cell in a honeycomb."

"That's great." Peter was impressed. "Let's find some more pennies, for a bigger square that will make a bigger hex thing."

"I guess you'd need an awful lot of pennies." Charlie shook his head. "Maybe I can figure it out."

How many pennies would be needed to carry out the same routine on the next bigger scale, the coins all flat on the table and packed as before?

41. SO VERY SIMPLE

Charlie handed back the sheet of paper. "Come on, that's an enormous number," he declared. "You can't expect me to multiply it by twenty-nine in my head."

"Why not? It's easy if you know how." Mike chuckled. "You only have to write the same extra digit at each end. And it's the smallest number that works that way for twenty-nine."

What was Mike's number?

42. POWER PLAY

Harry had been quiet for quite a while, busy with his homework. "Look, Dad," he said suddenly, holding up a sheet of paper. "I've figured out something about those three numbers."

Bruce looked. "That's our own house number, and your Aunt Jane's, and Uncle Tom's," he commented. "But what's all the figuring?"

"It connects them," replied the boy. "The square of ours is twice the cube of Aunt Jane's number, and it's three times the fifth power of Uncle Tom's."

It was hardly regular homework, but the boy was right. What were those numbers?

43. THE COLLECTOR

Walt was busy with his stamps when Jill looked in at his place. "I saw you coming out of Bretts last week," she said. "Did you find any bargains?"

"Nothing very special, but I did buy quite a lot—stamps I needed to complete certain sets," her brother replied.

"Just one hundred in all, and at four prices: 59¢, $1.99, $2.87 and $3.44 each."

"A lot of money," Jill commented. "How much?"

Walt smiled. "One hundred bucks exactly, and I guess I couldn't really afford it."

How many had he bought at each price?

44. A MATTER OF SQUARES

Charlie stopped outside the entrance. "Anyway it does have an interesting number," he commented. "Quite unique, in fact."

"Looks very ordinary to me." Greg shook his head. "But you know how I am about figures."

"Deplorable in a man of your age!" Charlie smiled. "But I'll tell you. If you total the squares of its three digits you'll get exactly half that number."

What was the number?

45. THE ONLY TREE

George took out his little book. "Let's have the number of your new house," he said. "I drove through your road yesterday, but I couldn't remember the number."

Steve smiled. "I guess they all look much the same, but we've got the only big tree in the development."

"I noticed it," George told him. "So you're on the north side."

"That's right, all even numbers are on our side," Steve replied. "But you figure it out yourself. All the even numbers above ours total half the sum of the even numbers below ours, and we've got a 2-figure number."

What was it, then?

46. IT MAKES SENSE

If one two one
    plus two one two
Is three times
    forty-three,
Then what can one
    one one plus one
One one plus
    one one be?

47. GRANDAD'S BIRTHDAY

"Don't be late now," said Susan. "Your grandfather's coming over. It's his birthday, you know."

Doug nodded. "Sure, and I made up something on his age. If you add up all the ages I've been, including my age now, you get one year more than his age," he replied. "And the total of the two figures of his age is my age."

What were the two ages?

48. VANDALISM

"I saw that some crazy kook broke into Jake's pet shop and opened some of the cages," said Martha. "He had just 300 birds there and more than 100 escaped."

"Too bad, they'll mostly die out on their own," Fred replied, checking in his newspaper. "They say a third of what remained were finches, a quarter budgies, a fifth canaries, a seventh mynah birds, and a ninth were parrots. And the original number of canaries was three times the number of parrots that remained."

Stupid vandalism! But one of those fractions was wrong. How many canaries escaped?

49. TRANSPORTATION

Sam shook his head. "It's quite a stretch, twenty-four miles to Tulla. But I can only take ten of you, all the truck will carry."

Greg thought a moment. "That's okay, we'll relay," he declared. "There are thirty of us, and it's essential we all arrive at the same time and as soon as possible. I could figure out the way if I knew what speed you'll drive."

The old man chuckled. "She's old and slow. It's a steady drop all the way there, so we'll do forty miles per hour. But coming back, uphill on that road, we'll only make thirty miles per hour."

"Fine." Greg had been jotting down some figures. "Some of us can start on foot and be picked up along the way. We walk at four miles per hour, so we'll all walk and ride."

Assuming truck and walkers all started at the same time, how long would it take the party to reach Tulla?

50. JUST FOR FUN

Walt was scribbling on a scratch pad. "Remember that teaser about a phone number?" he asked. "Well, I've made one about our new number."

"I remember. Something about the 3-digit exchange and the old 4-digit part, but I forget the details," his partner replied. "What have you figured out?"

"Look." Walt pointed. "If you subtract the exchange part from half the square of the other bit you get the complete 7-digit number again."

What was it?

51. GOOD SERVICE

"We have a fine commuter service here," said Steve. "Trains to your station all day long, and by two different routes."

"Sounds good," Fred commented. "What times do they run?"

"The first train via Poole leaves at 6:00 a.m., followed throughout the day by trains at regular intervals. Going via Tulla, the first is at 6:05 a.m., also followed throughout the day by trains at regular intervals," Steve replied. "They continue like that right through until soon after midnight on both routes. But it's odd that departures coincide only twice, the first time when the nineteenth Poole train and the eighteenth Tulla leave here simultaneously."

The "regular intervals" were exact numbers of minutes, so what were the two times of simultaneous departure?

52. BOTH HANDS

"I'm bored. Give me something to do," said Joe. "And what's the time anyway?"

Ben glanced at his watch and did some quick figuring. "When I checked my watch this morning," he replied, "the hour hand was exactly where the minute hand is now, and the minute hand was one division before where the hour hand is now."

"You mean minute division?" Joe asked.

"That's right," Ben told him. "And both hands are exactly at minute divisions now."

What was the time?

53. LONG ODDS

Pat picked up part of the deck of cards, and examined them. "Okay," he said. "Don't look, but draw three cards from these in my hand."

Jack complied, turning each card face up as he drew it. "All spades," he commented. "That's funny."

"It sure is," Pat agreed. "In fact the odds were exactly 11 to 2 against you getting three spades."

How many cards had Pat picked up from the deck, and how many had been spades?

54. THE TALKATIVE GUEST

"What a blabbermouth!" Ian exclaimed, watching as the car turned out of the driveway. "Did you get his story?"

"About four clients of his: a banker, a curate, an actor and a dentist." Sally smiled. "He called them Doug, Clem, Andy and Ben. But I never got which was which."

"I did better," her husband declared. "Doug's the dentist if Ben is the banker, but he's the actor if Andy's the curate. Ben is not the actor unless Doug's the dentist. Ben's the banker if Clem's the actor. Then Doug is the curate unless either Clem is the dentist or Ben's the banker, and anyway the curate is not Ben."

Ian was quite right! You figure it out.

55. URANIUM TRIANGLES

Tom's old gardener greeted me as I walked down the long driveway toward the house. "What's that you've made?" I asked him. "Looks like two new flower beds, but they're big."

"That's right," Sam replied. "It's something he got from a book. He says they're uranium triangles, with all sides exact numbers of feet and both areas exact square feet."

"You mean Heronian." I smiled. "An old guy who lived about two thousand years ago. He was quite a mathematician. But what are the exact dimensions of your triangles?"

"Well, their areas are the same." The old chap grinned. "Each of them has one side seventeen feet and another side twenty-eight feet. But their third sides are different, so maybe you can figure them out."

You try.

56. MEN ON THE MOON

"What's a moon crawler, Dad?" asked Elsie, looking up from her magazine.

"A special sort of truck with huge tires," Steve told her. "They're being used on the moon. Why do you ask?"

"It's mentioned here," the girl replied. "They're going to cross the Mare Hunticus. I guess that's all sand, and it's just 528 miles wide."

"Well, that's okay for a crawler if it carries enough fuel," Steve commented. "But I don't imagine it can carry very much."

Elsie smiled. "That's why I asked," she said. "It says a moon crawler carries enough fuel for only 315 miles in all, so I don't see how it could do the trip."

"What about setting up its own fuel caches en route?" Her father was thinking. "That's it, so let's figure out the minimum total mileage they would have to do to make the crossing.

You try!

57. A FRIENDLY TELLER

Susan emptied her purse onto the table. "It's crazy!" she exclaimed. "I had only $1.25 before we cashed my refund check at the bank. Now I've got exactly double the amount of the check."

Steve checked. "You're in luck. But don't blame me. We've been nowhere else."

"It must have been the teller," Susan told him. "Let's go back."

"Okay," her husband replied. "I know what she did. She gave you dollars for cents and cents for dollars, and she also reversed the order of the digits for each."

He was right, so what was the amount of the check?

58. MANY A MICKLE

"Some people make good beggars," said Bob, scanning the listed totals of the donations collected by his little band of helpers. Each year he and a few close friends devote much time to getting what they can from their acquaintances for the eleven charities that they support.

"Good?" Alan chuckled, pointing to the list. "Look at

those first two totals: 24¢ and $1.22. I'd call that beggarly beggary!"

Bob smiled. "My brother made out the list, and those were what his two kids collected. He put them in separately just for fun. But after the $1.22 entry every total is exactly double the previous one on the list, and that's an amazing coincidence."

"It sure is," his friend agreed. "I see you deduct only $52.00 altogether for expenses, and then you can divide the balance exactly equally among your charities."

How much would each charity receive?

59. A TALE OF WOE

Walter shook his head. "I closed down last week, and I'm broke," he said. "The last day we took in precisely $5.33, and that was the end."

"I'm sorry." Andy was shocked. "You started well, with good sales the first day and people standing in line."

"Maybe too well. Every day after that we took in less," Walter told him. "It was uncanny, like a curse. The second day we took in just one cent more than two-thirds of the first day's take, the third day two cents more than two-thirds of the second day, the fourth day three cents more than two-thirds of the third day, and so on. Each day another penny more than two-thirds of the previous day."

He had a real problem, and so will you if you want to solve this! How much had Walter taken the first day?

60. QUITE A FAMILY

"It's funny about Ben's five kids," said John, blessing the inane commercials that do provide some respite for conversation. "Not that we'd want five."

"I certainly wouldn't." Ann laughed. "But what's so odd about them?"

"Something I noticed today about their ages," replied her husband. "They're all different. The three boys are spaced two years apart, and the girls are too. And the squares of the boys' ages total exactly the difference between the cubes of the girls' ages."

Ann shook her head, turning back to the TV. That at least demanded no thinking!

What were the five ages?

61. NUMBERS, NUMBERS

Stan put down his pen. "I found something funny about your license number," he said. "It's one more than what you get if you add together the squares of its two halves. Look, Dad."

John looked. "That's the first three figures and the last three, eh? 403 and 491. Do you get 403490 if you total their squares?"

"Sure," replied the boy. "But d'you think there are any other 6-figure numbers that work that way?"

See you many you can find!

62. THE YEARS THAT COUNT

Sam stood the photo up again on his desk. "Yes, that's the whole family, just the four of us."

"Very nice too." Peter nodded. "I met your younger boy when he came in today with your wife. He told me he's nine, but I guess your other son is quite a bit older."

"That's right," Sam agreed. "It's odd about all our ages. If you total the squares of the boys' ages and mine, you get my wife's age multiplied by the total of my age and their two ages. All in complete years, of course."

Peter saw what he meant, but never managed to figure out those ages. What were they?

63. A FUNNY FRACTION

Mike pointed to an invoice that had come in the mail. "That's an odd amount," he said. "If you shift the cents and put them before the dollars you get just five-eighths of it in cents."

Charlie looked, and did some figuring on the back of an envelope. "That's right," he declared. "I guess it's the smallest amount that works that way."

He was right too, so what was the amount?

64. TWO MAGIC SQUARES

We have two regular Magic Squares.

Each entails a checkerboard-style array of positive consecutive numbers in square formation. Each row, each column, and each main diagonal must add up to the same magic total.

The magic totals are the same, and in each square 54 is the greatest number. Yet the Magic Squares are not the same!

What must their respective smallest numbers be?

65. THE JOKER'S WILD

Jack riffled the cards expertly. "Let's try something different today," he said.

"Okay." Bob smiled. "What's the idea?"

"Simple," his friend replied. "At the end of each game the loser pays exactly a third of the cash he's got then."

It sounded fair enough, so the two started playing. But after a while Jack pushed back his chair. "That's it," he declared. "You've now got precisely three times what I have, and I've lost almost exactly four bucks. And you won each of the last few games."

"Just luck. You won every game before those," Bob reminded him. "In fact we've both won the same number of games."

How much did each have when they started?

66. EASY COME EASY GO

This was one of the times Bill found it hard to keep his temper in the face of his partner's peculiarities. But most of the money was Ben's, and things did seem to work out right in spite of everything.

"So you order a lot of socks at $1.35 a pair," he commented. "Maybe five hundred dollars worth for all I know, but you have no idea how much exactly or how many."

Ben smiled. "That's right, except I didn't spend that much," he said, sprawled in his chair quite at ease in that rather absurd situation. "You worry too much about details, and there'll be an invoice. But I did notice when the guy wrote it down that the number of dollars in the total was three more than the square of the number of cents. That was without any tax or discount."

How many pairs had he ordered?

67. A BUG IN A BARN

When Tom looked into his long barn he found Bob busy with a measuring tape. "What's going on?" he asked.

"Checking what our teacher said," replied the boy. "Say a roach ran from that door to the other one, touching the front and back walls on the way, how far would his shortest possible route be?"

Tom smiled. "Beyond me," he said. "I guess it must depend on the dimensions."

"That's right." Bob glanced at the bit of paper in his hand. "The barn is thirty-two feet, front to back, and ninety feet long. That door at this end is thirteen feet from the back, and the door at the other end is eleven feet from the front, taking the middle of each."

What do you say?

68. WRONG NUMBER

"I'll have to get my number changed," said Joe. "I'm called at all hours, but it's never my number they want."

"That's tough." Mike nodded sympathetically. "Must be some number very like yours."

"Too darned like, although actually just three times my number. I found out it's a girls' residence, to do with the university. Me, of all old sinners!" Joe laughed. "If you shift the third figure of my number and put it first, and then close up the other three figures you get the number of that hen hovel."

So what was his number?

69. AT THE SHOW

Keith handed back the program. "I don't like going to a show in such a big group, but I guess you got a special rate."

"Sure, but we really weren't that many. If the whole club had gone there would have been getting on for a hundred," replied Ann. "They gave us one complete row, and we all drew for seats. Marilyn and I got the very end seats at opposite ends. The five Barton boys had come and one of them sat beside me."

"You liked that." Her father chuckled. "It's funny, the odds were exactly 2 to 1 against there being a girl at each end."

How many were there in the group?

70. THE PENALTY CLAUSE

"You know those old rose standards you want dug up," said Peter. "I'll tender for the job."

"Okay, son." His father laughed. "What's your offer?"

The boy was ready. "I get thirty-seven cents for each, and I'll do the lot in not more than two hours."

"I'll buy that," declared his father. "But you'll pay a penalty if you exceed the two hours. There's nearly ninety of them in all. For the first minute over the time you'll pay a penny, for the second minute two cents, for the third minute three cents, and so on. Part of a minute counts as a minute."

So Peter started, his father checking the time very carefully. And, when the job was done, Peter agreed that a net amount of $7.00 was due to him.

How many rose standards were there?

71. CONSECUTIVE SQUARES

Tony looked up when his father came in. "See this, Dad," he said, holding out a sheet of paper. "That's a very special number."

"Seven digits, and it ends with 6789," Sam commented. But that doesn't make it special. There are lots of numbers with 6789 as ending."

"Sure there are," Tony agreed. "But this one is also the sum of the squares of three consecutive numbers. I just figured it out."

The boy was right, so what was his number?

72. THINK OF A NUMBER

Harry smiled as his wife searched her bag angrily. "You drag me here to buy expensive paving stones, and then you don't know how many you need." he said. "Surely you can remember."

"Of course not." Fran shook her head. "That's why I wrote it down. But I do recall noticing the paved area was to be exactly seven times some other number in square feet."

"Most helpful if you hadn't forgotten that key number too." Harry chuckled. "But I'll tell you something. The bit of lawn is just eighteen feet by twenty-three, and the paved area will be less than it."

The complete patio was going to be square, with the stones laid out around the grass. What was the key number Fran had forgotten?

73. A DEAL IN STAMPS

"More stamps?" asked Connie, finding her husband busy at the table. "But I guess there are worse hobbies."

"I'm glad you feel that way." Rick looked up, smiling. "I just blew about thirty-two bucks on these two lots."

Connie picked up a stamp. "That's pretty," she said. "Any special bargains?"

"Not really, not at those prices, but it's funny how the prices came out," Rick replied. "For that lot I averaged as many cents each as the number of stamps in the lot. This smaller lot cost me three dollars and nineteen cents less, but they averaged five times as many cents each as the number in this lot."

His wife shook her head. That wasn't her hobby either. Maybe you can figure out the details.

74. A SERIAL NUMBER

Peter put down his pen. "You remember that old dollar bill you gave me, Dad?" he asked. "It's got an interesting serial number."

"So you didn't spend it yet." Tom glanced at the bill lying there on the table. "Eight digits, and I see the first and last digits are the same. Is that what you call interesting?"

"Come on, Dad, I'm not that stupid." The boy grinned. "Look. The complete number is exactly the fifth power of what you get when you write those first and last digits side by side."

What was the serial number?

75. AN EVENING OUT

Fiona followed her husband into the living room. "It was a lovely evening," she said. "But you must have spent about a hundred bucks."

"Not that much, and anyway you don't have a birthday so often." Stan was checking his cash on the table. "You know, I've still got a third as much as I had when we went out."

"Then you can afford this," Fiona told him, picking up two quarters. "That pays back what I gave the hat check girl."

Stan smiled. "Okay. Now I've got as many cents in coins as I had dollars in bills, and half as many dollars in bills as I had cents in coins."

How much did he have left?

76. A MATTER OF AGES

"That's good of you and Pat," said Bob, picking up a little photo on his colleague's desk. "But who's the other man?"

Ted smiled. "That's my son," he replied. "Robin. Maybe you'll meet him now he's back home for a while."

Bob examined the photo more closely. "I'll take your word for it, but you must have started young!"

"Come on." Ted chuckled. "The cube of Pat's age is the difference between the squares of Rob's age and mine, so you see he's not so old."

"No logic in that." Bob shook his head. "Just words."

Ted sighed. "Okay. My age is exactly in the same ratio to Rob's as his is to Pat's, and I've taken all three in complete years."

What were the three ages?

77. DROPPING IN ON LEN

Peter pointed to the map. "We're there, exactly midway between Ablin and Brent as the crow flies, and the same distance from Crowe," he said. "All dead straight roads too."

"Sure." Joe nodded. "And Len's place is just a third of the way along the straight highway from Ablin to Crowe.

Of course we'll go through Ablin. We're only twenty-three miles from him that way."

"That's right," Peter told him. "And each leg will be an exact number of miles."

Indeed it's an exact number of miles from Brent to Crowe. How many, then?

78. CARDS ON THE TABLE

"I thought you were playing solitaire," said Susan, looking up from her book. "Why all the cussing?"

"The table's too small." Len laughed. "Or maybe the cards are too big, even though they are the regular two and one-quarter by three and a half inches."

"So the furniture's wrong!" His wife smiled. "What's the game?"

"Just an idea. I want to lay out a whole deck of cards, fifty-two of them, edge to edge without overlapping or projecting beyond the table," Len replied. "But I can't fit them all in, and I'm left with a few clubs and the same number of hearts. Unfortunately it's the only rectangular table we have."

"That's right," Susan agreed. "One inch longer than it is wide."

"I know." Len was jotting down some figures. "I've still got eleven and one-quarter inches of waste space, arranging the cards the best way I can."

What were the dimensions of the tabletop?

79. A BUS RIDE

There were fewer than sixty of us passengers in the bus when it left Sam's terminus.

At Benton, the first stop, a third of the passengers got off, and five got on. At the next stop, again a third got off but only two got on. At the third stop half got off and four came aboard. And at the fourth stop half got off but only one boarded the bus. Of course, nobody re-entered the bus after alighting.

Dorling was the fifth stop, the end of the run. Handing Sam my $2.50 fare as I stepped down, I remarked on his rates. "Only 50 cents per stage, and half price for kids," I said. "You'll go broke!"

The old chap grinned. "It's enough for me. This trip the total take was exactly as many dollars as the total number of passengers, and just one-fifth of them were kids at the low rate."

How many adult passengers had there been?

80. YOU'RE SURE IF IN DOUBT

Ted sipped his drink appreciatively, glancing around the cozy living room. "All the same, as I recall it last time I saw you four years ago. How old are your two kids now?"

"Three, not two. Pam's had another meanwhile." Charlie smiled. "If you multiply their three ages you get ninety-six, but they add up to the number of this house."

"You're smart," Ted told him. "But that still doesn't tell me for sure."

His friend chuckled. "Sure it does. Just think."

What do you make those ages?

81. CREEPY CRAWLIES

"Slugs?" Tom chuckled. "I got rid of them in my backyard, and none of those chemical killers."

"We're infested with them," his friend told him. "What did you do?"

"Simple and cheap," Tom replied. "I made a deal with our kids and the kids next door. Each would get a dime for every slug he collected, but each would pay me three cents each for all the slugs collected by the other kids in the gang."

Andy smiled. "Quite a scheme, but it doesn't sound so very cheap for you."

"It was," Tom declared. "In fact it cost me an average of exactly ninety-five cents for each of the gang."

How many slugs were collected?

82. FAMILY NUMBERS

Doug was busy at the table. "Say, Dad. Is Aunt Elsie's phone number 9638?" he asked. "And Uncle Fred's number 2591?"

"That's right, and don't forget ours is 8739 if you're listing family numbers," replied Steve. "Is that it?"

"No, but something I just figured out about those three numbers," the boy replied. "Each of them gives exactly the same remainder when you divide by one special number I discovered."

What was that special number?

83. TOO MANY GIRLS

"What's new with the checkers tournament at school?" Clem asked. "You did tell me you'd lost one game against some girl."

"All finished, Dad," replied Jack. "Everyone had to play everyone else once. Mike and I were the only guys, and the girls all did better than either of us. Between us he and I scored only nine points in all."

"So you played left-handed." His father chuckled. "How were points counted?"

"One for a win, half a point for a draw," the boy told him. "It was funny the girls all got exactly the same number of points."

How many girls were in the tournament?

84. WHAT? NO ZOBBLIES?

Mike missed the gurgling gluck-glucks and grumphs of the zobblies when he went into his little pet shop. "What happened to those Venus toads?" he asked his wife. "Don't say you sold them all."

"Sure did. Exactly a hundred of them for exactly twenty bucks," Susan replied. "I knew the kids would go for them at those prices. Ninety-seven cents for five, sixty-seven cents for three, or singly at a quarter each."

Amazing! Only a few years ago man had not even reached the Moon! How many of those creatures had Susan sold singly?

85. THE CENSUS

They've counted the cats in Llanfair,
Which number a third of a square.
If a quarter were slain,
Just a cube would remain.
How many, at least, must be there?

86. A WHIZ KID

"Nothing to it, eh? Well, I'd say exactly a seventh of the questions are really tough, so we'll make a deal." Charlie chuckled. "I'll give you 7¢ for every one you get right. But you'll pay me a penny for the first mistake, 2¢ for the second, 3¢ the third, and so on. Any question you don't answer counts as a mistake."

John grinned. "Fine, Dad," he said, reaching for the quiz sheet. "It'll cost you!"

In fact, the boy answered more than three-quarters of the questions correctly, but he made only $1.68 on the deal.

How many questions were there?

87. TICKETS IN THE SWEEP

"A kid from the school was here selling tickets for your draw," said Susan. "I took three."

"That's fine, Mom," Jack told her. "But Jill and I each got a ticket already. There are a thousand in all, so let's see what your numbers are."

Susan handed him her tickets from the dresser. "You see they're consecutive numbers. Let Jill keep them, they'll be safer with her."

Jack ignored that remark! "It's funny about these," he declared. "The square of your lowest number added to the square of mine is the square of your highest, and that's also the square of your middle number added to the square of Jill's."

What were the five numbers?

88. PROGRESS

Ben put down his glass. "I see you're going to have a high-rise on Tulla Trail," he said. "Will it bother you?"

"We're okay. It's well up the road on the other side," Joe replied. "They're the odd numbers."

"Lucky for you," Ben commented. "What numbers are involved?"

Joe smiled. "It's funny about that. They bought a block of adjoining houses running up to No. 43, their highest number. And I noticed that the sum of the numbers in that block is exactly equal to the sum of all the other numbers that side below and above the ones they bought."

What numbers were bought?

89. THREE TIMES

Stan walked over to where his son was writing at the table. "Busy?" he asked.

"Not really, Dad," Bill replied. "I just found something special about this number. If you move its final pair of digits and put them in front of the others you multiply the number by three."

"That's odd." Stan looked down at the boy's working. "Will there be other numbers like that?"

Bill nodded. "Sure, but you said 'odd,' and this is the smallest odd number that works that way for three times."

What was Bill's number?

90. A TOUCHING TALE

Tom stopped at the gate. "That's my little field," he said. "Exactly square, all fences in good shape."

"Seems just what I want, but I'll check that fence," Andy replied. "What was the area?"

"You like teasers." Tom chuckled. "We're forty-eight feet from that fence, and the other gate in the side opposite us is one hundred and sixty-eight feet from it. If you want to touch that fence on your way to the other gate, going right up to it, you'll have to go at least forty-eight feet further than the direct route from where we are."

What was the area?

91. FUN FOR SOME

"One of your problems?" Martha asked, finding her husband busy at the desk. "I don't know what you see in them."

Jack smiled. "Maybe you will when you reach my age," he replied. "Now I've figured out something on our ages. If you write my age after yours, the 4-figure number will be twice the square of your age subtracted from three times the square of mine."

Just for fun! But what were their ages?

92. HE BROKE THE BANK

Mary smiled, seeing the sorry mess on the rug. "So that's the end of your ugly old piggy bank," she said. "Was there much in it?"

"Quite a bit, but it's funny the way it was," her husband replied. "The dimes, nickels and quarters were all prime numbers. And there were as many pennies as the number of dimes multiplied by the total nickels and dimes."

"What about quarters?" Mary asked.

Stan grinned. "A good question, but figure it out yourself. There were 288 more pennies than quarters, and no other money of course."

How much was there in all?

93. DO IT YOURSELF

"Holy mackerel!" exclaimed Steve, viewing the litter on the floor as he stood in the doorway. "What's broken?"

"Getting on for fifteen hundred little tiles," Joe told him. "You remember my two blackwood Chinese tables with little square tiles covering the tops? They had dry rot, so I decided to use all those identical tiles for two new tables."

"Sure, they were exactly the same with square tops." His friend nodded. "Will the new tables be identical too?"

Joe shook his head. "Square tops, but they were going to be different sizes. One would have been twenty-three tiles, and I would have had exactly the right total to cover both tops completely. But one damned table collapsed just as I finished stripping it, and all its tiles were shattered."

Steve picked up some fragments. "Fine ceramic, too bad," he commented. "What'll you do?"

"Use what I have left," Joe replied. "Oddly enough they'll provide square tops for two smaller tables without wasting any, though one will be rather small."

How many tiles did he have left?

94. A BUG FOR THE BIRDS

The three sparrows perched expectantly at their respective corners of the square bird feeder. "D'you see the big fat bug on that flower, level with this tray?" asked Pippy. "It's still sixty-five inches from me, so I'll wait for it to come nearer."

Peppy, diagonally opposite from her, replied instantly. "Sure. It's only thirty-seven inches from me, but it may come right on to this feeder tray if we're patient."

The third bird was hungry. "Why wait?" he asked. "It's fifty-one inches from me, and I guess it's asleep."

The tray was flat. What was its size?

95. A LUCKY NUMBER

"So you fell for the lottery too," said Ron, glancing at the ticket. "But I don't see anything special about your number. What makes 109989 so lucky?"

Jim smiled. "Look again," he replied. "If you multiply it by nine you get exactly the same digits in reversed order."

Ron checked. "That is funny, but you can probably find another 6-figure number that works the same way with a different 1-digit number."

Can you?

96. A MATTER OF TIME

Andy looked up when his partner came in. "I tried to get you yesterday afternoon," he said. "They told me you'd gone out early, but you weren't back when I left."

"That's right. I did drop in on my way home but you'd just gone." Greg replied. "So here's a little teaser for you. When I came back the minute hand was right on a minute mark exactly where the hour hand had been when I went out, and the hour hand was just two minutes ahead of where the minute hand had been."

What time had he come back that afternoon?

97. THE POSTER

"You know that old Swiss railway poster you gave me, Dad?" said Peter. "Just now I folded it once, putting one corner on top of the opposite corner. The fold was exactly 136 centimeters long."

Charlie smiled. "So what? It was a big poster," he replied. "I do recall it was 120 centimeters wide to fit a promotion display I was arranging, but I don't remember how long it was."

What was its length?

98. AT THE CASINO

They had been standing at the crowded roulette table, watching as the little white ball clicked its erratic way to a final stop in each spin of the big black wheel. "One number has come up twice in the short time we've been here," said Alan. "Did you notice?"

Jim smiled. "Sure, but it could happen quite often," he replied. "With the regular 36 numbers plus a single zero as they have here, the odds are almost exactly 3 to 1 against getting the same number at least twice in the number of spins we've watched."

How many spins was that?

99. NO DIRECT ROAD

"Yes, I do my shopping at Poole, even though it is eight miles from me as the crow flies," said Beryl. "Just a matter of access."

Sam nodded. "That's why we see you so often. But aren't Alton and Bray both nearer to you?" he asked. "I know the three villages are equal distances from each other, making a triangle."

"Sure, but that's what I mean," Beryl replied. "I'm only three miles from Bray and five miles from Alton, but there's no direct road to either."

How far apart were the three villages?

100. A NEST EGG

"That's right, a sort of trust fund. I started it on Mary's first birthday with a deposit that was the product of her age and her mother's in dollars," said Geoffrey. "Got the idea thinking about the coincidence that they have the same birthday. And every birthday since then I've done the same, the new product of their ages."

Dick smiled. "A great idea, and it could be a very handy nest egg for the future. How much is the fund now?"

"I'm not sure exactly, what with interest," Geoffrey replied. "But so far I've deposited just $888 in all."

How old was her mother when Mary was born?

SOLUTIONS TO TEASERS

1. PECKING ORDER

Say there were x seeds.

Pip left $\dfrac{2x - 4}{3}$, Pep left $\dfrac{4x - 20}{9}$, Pop left $\dfrac{8x - 76}{27}$.

Then, Pep took $\dfrac{2x + 8}{9}$.

Pap took $2 + \dfrac{8x - 130}{81}$, i.e., $\dfrac{8x + 32}{81}$.

So $\dfrac{8x + 32}{81} = \dfrac{x + 4}{9} - 2$, whence $x = 158$.

They started with 158 seeds in the dish.

2. FOR THE ONE THAT GOT AWAY

Say Clem bought y lures at x cents each.

Then he sold them at $x(x + 100)/100 = y^2$ cents each.

Hence, $x^2 + 100x = 100y^2$, so say $x = 10z$.

Thence, $(z + 5)^2 - y^2 = 25$.

Tabulating for factors:
$$
\begin{aligned}
(z + 5) + y &= 25 \\
(z + 5) - y &= 1 \\
\hline
(z + 5) &= 13 \\
y &= 12
\end{aligned}
$$

Hence, $z = 8$, making $x = 80$, with $y = 12$.

So Clem bought 12 lures at 80 cents apiece, and sold them at \$1.44 each.

3. LONG ODDS

Say there were $(x + 4)$ cards in all, including the four aces.

Then the chance of drawing the four aces was:
$$\frac{4}{x + 4} \cdot \frac{3}{x + 3} \cdot \frac{2}{x + 2} \cdot \frac{1}{x + 1} = \frac{1}{1001}.$$

$4 \cdot 3 \cdot 2 \cdot 1 = 24.$

Hence, as a very rough approximation, $x^4 = 24000$ (not more).

So, as a very rough approximation, $x^2 = 154$ (not more).

Thence, again as a very rough approximation, $x = 12$ (not more).

Now, $1001 = 7 \cdot 11 \cdot 13$, and all of $(x + 4)$, $(x + 3)$, $(x + 2)$, and $(x + 1)$ must be factors of 1001.

Then, regarding that requirement concerning factors, none of $(x + 4)$, $(x + 3)$, $(x + 2)$, or $(x + 1)$ can be a multiple of 5. Hence we must have $x = 10$.

There were 14 cards on the table, including the four aces.

4. LIKE FATHER LIKE SON

Ages: Sam $(10x + y)$, Mike $(10a + b)$.

Then, $(x + y + a + b)^2 = 2(10x + y + 10a + b) - 1$
  and $(x + y)^2 - (10x + y) = (a + b)^2 - (10a + b)$.

Say: $x + y = m$, making $10x + y = 9x + m$
  and $a + b = n$, making $10a + b = 9a + n$.

Then, $n^2 - (9a + n) = m^2 - (9x + m)$,
  whence $(m - n)(m + n - 1) = 9(x - a)$.

Also, $(m + n)^2 = 2(m + n + 9x + 9a) - 1$,
  so $(m + n)(m + n - 2) = 18(x + a) - 1$,
  which makes $(m + n)$ odd, and therefore $(m - n)$ odd.
  Also, since $(m + n - 1)$ will be even, $(x - a)$ is even.

We had $(m - n)(m + n - 1) = 9(x - a)$.

Tabulate for possible even $(x - a)$ values, noting that $m < 19$.

$x - a$	$=$	2		4		6	8
$9(x - a)$	$=$	18		36		54	72
$m + n - 1$	$=$	6	18	12	36	18	24
$m - n$	$=$	3	1	3	1	3	3
$m + n$	$=$	7	19	13	37	19	25
m	$=$	5	10	8	—	11	14
n	$=$	2	9	5	—	8	11
$m + n - 2$	$=$	5	17	11	—	17	23
$(m + n)(m + n - 2)$	$=$	35	323	143	—	323	575
making $18(x + a)$	$=$	36	324	144	—	324	576
whence $x + a$	$=$	2	18	8	—	18	—
and $x - a$	$=$	2	2	4	—	6	—
so x	$=$	2	—	6	—	—	—
with y	$=$	3	—	2			
and a	$=$	0	—	2			
with b	$=$	2	—	3			
Sam's age	$=$	23	—	62			
Mike's age	$=$	2	—	23			

Obviously the ages 23 and 2 cannot be acceptable, hence Sam was 62 years old, and Mike 23. Ann was 2 years old.

5. WHO SPILLED THE COFFEE?

Say x knives at \$2.96, y as the first digit of the dollars and z as the last digit of the cents in the amount.

Then, $296x = 100000y + z + 70490$, so $z = 4k + 2$, say.
But $z < 10$, hence $z = 2$ or 6.

With $z = 2$, we have $2(37x - 12500y) = 17623$, which is impossible because 3 is odd.
So $z = 6$, leading to $37x - 12500y = 8812$, with general solution: $x = 12500t + 576$, and $y = 37t + 1$.

Hence $x = 576, y = 1$.
The amount was \$1704.96 for 576 knives.

6. SO FAR APART

Say Sonia's 7-digit number was x, initial digit not zero, and Ted's 4-digit number y.
Then, $7x^3 = 3y^7 = 7^m 3^n p^{21}$, say.
Thence, $x^3 = 7^{m-1} 3^n p^{21}$, whence $m = 3a + 1, n = 3b$.
Also, $y^7 = 7^m 3^{n-1} p^{21}$, whence $m = 7c, n = 7d + 1$.

So, $3a + 1 = 7c$, entailing $c = 3k + 1, a = 7k + 2$, say,
and, $7d + 1 = 3b$, entailing $b = 7t - 2, d = 3t - 1$, say.
Thence, $m = 21k + 7, n = 21t - 6$.
So, $x = 7^{7k+2} \cdot 3^{7t-2} \cdot p^7, y = 7^{3k+1} \cdot 3^{3t-1} \cdot p^3$.

But, $y < 10000, 3^{3t-1} \geq 9, 7^{3k+1} \geq 7$, so $p = 1$ or 2.
Also, $7^9 > 10^8$, so we must have $k = 0$.
Then, since $y < 10000$, we must have $t = 1$ or 2.

Thence it is trivial to show that we must have:
$$x = 2^7 \cdot 3^5 \cdot 7^2 = 1524096, y = 2^3 \cdot 3^2 \cdot 7 = 0504.$$
Sonia's number was 1524096, Ted's was 0504.

7. ALL TWOS

Say the individual amounts in one invoice were:
x^2 dollars, x cents; y^2 dollars, y cents; z^2 dollars, z cents.
And assume $x > y > z$.
Then, $100x^2 + 100y^2 + 100z^2 + x + y + z = 22222$,
    so $x < 15$.
Thence, $(x + y + z) < 40$.
But we must have $(x + y + z - 22)$ divisible by 100,
    so $(x + y + z) = 22$, whence $z < 7$.
Also, $(x^2 + y^2 + z^2) = 222$.
Now try the possible values for z:

$z =$	1	2	3	4	5	6
$z^2 =$	1	4	9	16	25	36
making $x^2 + y^2 =$	221	218	213	206	197	186.

But $213 = 3 \cdot 71, 206 = 2 \cdot 103, 186 = 2 \cdot 3 \cdot 31$. So none of 213, 206 and 186 can be the sum of two squares, because each has a prime factor of form $(4r - 1)$.
Then: $221 = 10^2 + 11^2 = 5^2 + 14^2$,
    $218 = 7^2 + 13^2, 197 = 1^2 + 14^2$.
But we require $x + y + z = 22$.
$1 + 10 + 11 = 22, 2 + 7 + 13 = 22, 5 + 1 + 14 = 20$.

There were the two invoices, so the respective amounts were:

$121.11, $100.10, $1.01   for total $222.22
and $169.13, $ 49.07, $4.02   for total $222.22.

8. THOSE SHARES

Say the apportionment was: x, $\sqrt{xy}$, y; with $x \geq y$.

Then say $x = a^2c$, $y = b^2c$, $xy = abc$.
Thence, $c(a^2 + ab + b^2) = 409$. But 409 is prime, so $c = 1$.
Then $(a^2 + ab + b^2) = 409$
   whence $(2a + b)^2 + 3b^2 = 4 \cdot 409$.
We may obviously ignore the fact that $1^2 + 3 \cdot 1^2 = 4$,
   since $(2a + b)$ cannot equal 1 here.
So, say $(2a + b) = 2A$, and $b = 2B$, whence $A^2 + 3B^2 = 409$.

"At sight," $19^2 + 3 \cdot 4^2 = 409$, that being the unique
   representation since 409 is prime.
Hence we must have $A = 19$, $B = 4$, whence $a = 15$, $b = 8$.
So $x = 225$, $y = 64$.
The apportionment was 225, 120, and 64 shares.

9. YOU HAVE TO KNOW HOW

Say Tom's age was $(10x + y)$ years, Len's special digit z.
Then, $70x + 7y = 100y + 10z + x$, so $69x - 93y = 10z$.

Say $z = 3w$, whence $23x - 31y = 10w$.
Since x, y, and w are integers, that equation has the
   general solution:
$$w = 31k - 7x, \text{ with } y = 3x - 10k.$$

Obviously, since we require $w = 1, 2,$ or 3, with $y < 10$, we
   must have $k < 3$. With $k = 2$, we have $w > 3$.
But, with $k = 1$, we have $x = 4$, $y = 2$, $w = 3$.
Thence, $z = 9$, making Tom's age 42 years, Len's digit 9.

10. SAVINGS

Say x dimes, y nickels, z quarters, $(z + 24)$ pennies.
Then, $x(x + y) = z + 24$.

If $x = 2$, the only even prime number, then z would be even, which is impossible since $z \neq x$.
If $z = 2$, we would have $x(x + y) = 26 = 1 \cdot 26$ or $2 \cdot 13$, but 1 is not a prime number, so that is unacceptable.

So x and z are both odd primes.
Hence $(z + 24)$ is odd, whence $(x + y)$ is odd.
But $x \neq 2$, so y is even, hence $y = 2$.
Then $z + 24 = x^2 + 2x$, whence $z = (x + 6)(x - 4)$.
But z is prime, so we must have $(x - 4) = 1$, whence $x = 5$.
Thence $z = 11$.

So the money box contained 11 quarters, 5 dimes, 2 nickels and 35 pennies.

11. A RANDOM MAILING

Say he picked n cards, there being $20n$ cards in the index.
Then, successively he picked nos. 1, 3, 6, 10, 15, etc., in the card index.

So the final card that he picked was no. $\dfrac{n(n + 1)}{2}$.

But that was in fact the last card in the index.
So, since there were $20n$ cards in all, $n(n + 1) = 40n$, whence $n = 39$.
George picked 39 cards.

12. NO COMPUTER FOR THIS

Say $N = 10000x + y$. Then, $x^2 + y^2 = 30000x + 3y$.
Hence, $(2x - 30000)^2 + (2y - 3)^2 = 900000009 = 9 \cdot 17 \cdot 5882353 = 9 \cdot 5882353 \cdot (4^2 + 1^2)$.

We require a representation of 5882353 as the sum of two squares, say $(a^2 + b^2)$.
Then, $(10^4)^2 + 1^2 = (a^2 + b^2)(4^2 + 1^2)$
$$= (4a + b)^2 + (a - 4b)^2.$$
So we have: $(4a + b) = 10000$, with $(a - 4b) = \pm 1$, which has the solution: $a = 2353$, $b = 588$.

Then $100000001 = (2353^2 + 588^2)(4^2 + 1^2)$
$$= (9412 \pm 588)^2 + (2353 \mp 2352)^2$$
$$= 8824^2 + 4705^2 \text{ or } 10000^2 + 1^2.$$

There can be no representation of 3 as the sum of two
  squares, so we have $900000009 = 26472^2 + 14115^2$ or
  $30000^2 + 3^2$.
But x must have 4 digits, hence $(2x - 30000) \neq \pm 3000$.
So, $2x - 30000 = -26472$, with $2y - 3 = 14115$,
  whence $x = 1764$, $y = 7059$, making $N = 17647059$.

NOTE: It is not relevant in this particular problem, but
  in fact 5882353 is a prime number, hence there
  was no alternative value for N.

13. AT THE DINER

Until identified by name a girl will be shown as G, a man
  as M.
The seating arrangement includes two sequences:
  Ron, G, M, Joan; and Ann, M, G, M, G, Pam's husband.
But the girl to left of Pam's husband was not Pam, so
  must have been Joan.
Hence, sitting around the table, they were:
  Ann, Ron, Pam, M, Joan, Pam's husband.
But Steve sat on the right of the girl who sat on Harry's
  right. Hence the arrangement must have been:
  Ann, Ron, Pam, Harry, Joan, Steve.
Steve was Pam's husband.

14. THEY DON'T COME SINGLY

Check for x dollars and y cents, i.e., $(100x + y)$ ¢.
Each incorrect entry was for $(100y + x)$¢,
  so $(100x + y) - (200y + 2x) = \pm 1333$,
  whence $98x - 199y = \pm 1333$,
  with general integral solution:
  $$x = 199k - 40 \qquad x = 199k + 40$$
  $$\text{or}$$
  $$y = 98k - 13 \qquad y = 98k + 13$$
But we require $x < 100$, hence x 40, $y = 13$.
Check was for \$40.13.

15. WHO GLUBS GLYGONS?

Say they gathered x glygons, x being "nearly 1000."
Flab left $(3x - 12)/4$.

Finally, Flub left $(81x - 804)/256$.
So, $(81x - 804)/256 = 4y$, say.
Then $81x - 1024y = 804$, with integral solution:
$$x = 1024k - 28, y = 81k - 3.$$
But we require x "nearly 1000," so $x = 996$, with $y = 78$.
They gathered 996 glygons.

16. THREE IN A ROW

Say the ages were x, y and z years; all less than 10 years.
Then, $100x + 10y + z = 32(x + y + z)$,
  whence $68x - 22y = 31z$, so z is even.
Say $z = 2w$, making $34x - 11y = 31w$, with $w = 1, 2, 3,$ or 4.

Dividing by 11, we have $x = 11k - 2w$, $y = 34k - 9w$.
Now $2w < 10$, and $x < 10$, hence $11k < 20$,
  so we have $k = 1$.
Thence, $x = 11 - 2w$, $y = 34 - 9w$.
But $y < 10$, so $w > 2$.
Also we must have $9w < 34$, so $w < 4$.
Hence $w = 3$, with $x = 5$, $y = 7$, $z = 6$.

The ages, in the order in which Ray wrote them down, were 5, 7, and 6 years.

17. A SWITCH

Say the number was $(10000y + x)$, with $x < 10000$,
  $y < 1000$.
With the two parts "switched" it becomes $(1000x + y)$,
  so $1000x + y = 2(10000y + x) + 1$,
  whence $998x - 19999y = 1$.

Dividing through by 998, $(39y + 1)/998$ must be an integer.
In order to obtain a result such that $(y + t)/998$, say, will be an integer, we carry out the elementary arithmetic routine for finding the H.C.F. (i.e., Highest Common Factor) of two numbers:

```
    1 │ 39 │ 998 │ 25
      │ 23 │ 975 │
    2 │ 16 │  23 │ 1
      │ 14 │  16 │
      │  2 │   7 │ 3
      │    │   6 │
      │    │   1 │
```

Then the continued fraction $\dfrac{1}{25} + \dfrac{1}{1} + \dfrac{1}{1} + \dfrac{1}{2} + \dfrac{1}{3} = \dfrac{17}{435}$

So we multiply $(39y + 1)/998$ by 435, making

$\dfrac{16965y + 435}{998}$, which must be an integer. Thence,

$\dfrac{-y + 435}{998}$ is an integer, so $y = 435$, making $x = 8717$.

The phone number was 435-8717.

18. JUST TRIANGLES

Say sides of one triangle were $(x + y)$, $(x + z)$, $(y + z)$ inches.

Then area was $\sqrt{xyz(x + y + z)}$, perimeter $2(x + y + z)$, whence $9xyz = 16(x + y + z)$.

Now $\dfrac{xyz}{x + y + z} = \dfrac{16}{9}$. But, $\dfrac{3 \cdot 3 \cdot 3}{3 + 3 + 3} = \dfrac{27}{9}$,

so taking $x \geq y \geq z$, no solution is possible with $z > 2$.

Say $z = 1$. Then $9xy - 16x - 16y = 16$,
so $(9x - 16)(9y - 16) = 400$.
Taking factors for integral x and y:

$$9x - 16 = 200 \quad 20$$
$$9y - 16 = 2 \quad 20$$
$$x = 24 \quad 4$$
$$y = 2 \quad 4$$

So, sides: 26, 25, 3 and 8, 5, 5.

Say $z = 2$. Similarly we have $(9x - 8)(9y - 8) = 208$, giving $x = 24$, $y = 1$, with sides 26, 25, 3.

Hence there were only the two different triangles, with sides 26, 25, 3 inches and 8, 5, 5 inches.

19. AN ANCIENT PROBLEM

We have integers A, B, C such that $(A + B + C)$ is a square, and each of $(A + B)$, $(B + C)$, and $(A + C)$ is also a square. The great mathematician Diophantos developed the general integral solution for this problem about 1700 years ago.

Say $A + B + C = (x + y)^2$, $(A + B) = x^2$ with
$C = (2xy + y^2)$ and $(B + C) = (x - y)^2$.
Then, $B = (x^2 - 4xy)$, with $A = 4xy$, $C = (2xy + y^2)$.

We require $(A + C)$ to be square, so $(y^2 + 6xy) = z^2$, say, making $(3x)^2 + z^2 = (3x + y)^2$, which has the general integral solution:
$x = (m^2 - n^2)k$, $y = 6n^2k$, $z = 6mnk$,
m and n being any integers, k a common factor.

Thence: $A = 24n^2(m^2 - n^2)k^2$, $B = (m^2 - n^2)(m^2 - 25n^2)k^2$,
$C = 12n^2(m^2 + 2n^2)k^2$, $A + B + C = (m^2 + 5n^2)^2k^2$.

But for our particular problem we require values within the limits of human ages. Hence, re the expression for B, we must have $m > 5n$.
Then, observing that $(A + B + C) < 13$, quick trial of a very few (m, n) values gives the only acceptable solution with $m = 7$, $n = 1$, $k = 6$.
Thence $A = 32$, $B = 32$, $C = 17$.
Ages: Bessie 32 years, Joe 32, Peter 17, Sally 9.

20. SIMILAR BUT DIFFERENT

Say the triangles had sides ax, ay, az and bx, by, bz.
And say $ax = bz$, $az = by$.
Then, $z = ax/b = by/a$, so $x/y = b^2/a^2$.
Hence, $x = b^2k$, $y = a^2k$, $z = abk$, say.
Thence:
$$ax = ab^2k \quad bx = b^3k$$
$$ay = a^3k \quad by = a^2bk$$
$$az = a^2bk \quad bz = ab^2k$$
So, $(a^3 - b^3)k = 19$, which is prime, whence $k = 1$, making $a = 3$, $b = 2$.

The sides were: 12, 18 and 27 inches,
                    8, 12 and 18 inches.

21. JUST FOR KIDS

Stan bought $12x$ at $12x$ ¢, $12y$ at $12y$ ¢, $12z$ at $12z$ ¢, with $x > y > z$ say.
Total cost $144(x^2 + y^2 + z^2)$¢ for $12(x + y + z)$ hats at average price 50¢.

Hence, $144(x^2 + y^2 + z^2) = 600(x + y + z)$,
so $(12x - 25)^2 + (12y - 25)^2 + (12z - 25)^2 = 1875$.

$(12z - 25)^2 < (12y - 25)^2 < (12x - 25)^2$,
   so $(12z - 25)^2 < 625$, hence $z < 5$. Also $z > 2$.

With $z = 4$, $(12x - 25)^2 + (12y - 25)^2 = 1346 = 35^2 + 11^2$,
   making $x = 5$, $y = 3$, which is not acceptable because
   we require $y > z$.
Then, with $z = 3$, we have $y = 4$, and $x = 5$.

Stan bought 60 at 60¢, 48 at 48¢, 36 at 36¢, a total of 144
   hats.

22. THE PATIO

The ancient Heronian formula for the area of any triangle
   is:
$A = \sqrt{s(s - x)(s - y)(s - z)}$, where the sides are x, y, z,
   and $2s = x + y + z$.

Substituting for s, this makes:
$$16A^2 = [2yz + (x^2 - y^2 - z^2)][2yz - (x^2 - y^2 - z^2)]$$
$$= (2yz)^2 - (x^2 - y^2 - z^2)^2.$$

Here we have $x^2 = 196$, $y^2 = 97$, $z^2 = 41$,
   whence $16A^2 = 12544$, hence $A = 28$.
The area of the unpaved triangle was 28 square feet.

23. SQUARES AND SQUARES

Ages: Sam A, wife B, Jack y, house number x, all integral.
Then $x(y + 1) = 2A^2$, and $y(x + 1) = 2B^2$, which entails
   $x = 2a^2 = c^2 - 1$, and $y = 2b^2 = d^2 - 1$, say, where a, b,
   c, d are integers.
Then, $c^2 - 2a^2 = 1$, $d^2 - 2b^2 = 1$.
So the pairs (c, a) and (d, b) are particular pairs in the
   integral solution of $P^2 - 2Q^2 = 1$.

In that Pell equation all successive P, Q values are:
$$P = 1 \quad 3 \quad 17 \quad 99 \quad \text{etc.}$$
$$Q = 0 \quad 2 \quad 12 \quad 70 \quad \text{etc.,}$$
P and Q obeying the relation $U_{n+2} = 6U_{n+1} - U_n$.

Tabulate the first few values with corresponding x or y
    values:

$$P = c \text{ or } d = 1 \quad 3 \quad 17 \quad 99 \quad \text{etc.}$$
$$Q = a \text{ or } b = 0 \quad 2 \quad 12 \quad 70 \quad \text{etc.}$$
$$x \text{ or } y = 0 \quad 8 \quad 288 \quad 9800 \quad \text{etc.}$$

But y is the son's age, so $y = 8$, with $x = 288$, making A
    $= 36, B = 34$.

Sam's age was 36 years, his wife's, 34 years.

24. WRONG BUT RIGHT

Say the three amounts were x cents, y cents, z cents, with
    $x \geq y \geq z$. Then in dollars they were $x/100$, $y/100$, $z/100$.
Then the sum was $(x + y + z)/100$, the product $xyz/1000000$.
But the total was \$5.70, so $x + y + z = 570$, $xyz = 57 \cdot 10^5$.
Say $z = 100$, making $xy = 57000$, and $x + y = 470$, so
    $x(470 - x) = 57000$, whence $x^2 - 470x + 57000 = 0$,
    making $x = 235 \pm \sqrt{55225 - 57000}$, which is impossible.
Hence $z > 100$, and obviously $z < 190$.
Now, z must be a factor of $5700000 = 2^5 \cdot 3 \cdot 5^5 \cdot 19$, so z
    must be one of 114, 120, 125, 150, 152, 160.
Solving the corresponding quadratic in x for each possi-
    bility, in the same way as for the case of $z = 100$, we
    derive non-rational values for x in the cases of 114, 120,
    150, and 160. But with $z = 125$, we have $x = 285$, $y =$
    160; with $z = 160$, we have $x = 285$, $y = 125$, which is
    impossible since we require $y \geq z$.
So $x = 285, y = 160, z = 125$.
Prices: \$2.85, \$1.60, \$1.25.

25. THE STAMP

$(3 + 9 + 10 + 12 + 13 + 14) = 61 \equiv 1 \pmod 3$
The 5 stamps used at the airport totaled a multiple of 3
    kuks.
Hence the remaining stamp had to be of value $\equiv 1 \pmod 3$, so was for 10 kuks or 13 kuks.

Say 13 kuks: $(3 + 9 + 10 + 12 + 14) = 48 = 16 \cdot 3$,
    but no combination will give 16.
Say 10 kuks: $(3 + 9 + 12 + 13 + 14) = 51 = 17 \cdot 3$,
    and $3 + 14 = 17, 9 + 12 + 13 = 34$.

So the postcards took stamps for 17 kuks and 34 kuks. Andy retained the 10-kuk stamp.

26. A TALE OF TWO GUYS

Say the lengths of the wires were x and $(250 - x)$ feet, with $x > (250 - x)$, and the end of the shorter wire was y feet from the pole at the ground.

Then, $c^2 - 2a^2 = 1$, $d^2 - 2b^2 = 1$.

so $\sqrt{784 + (y + 150)^2} + \sqrt{784 + y^2} = 250$ (A)

But $[784 + (y + 150)^2] - [784 + y^2] = 300(y + 75)$,

so $\sqrt{784 + (y + 150)^2} - \sqrt{784 + y^2} = 6(y + 75)/5$ (B)

Subtracting (B) from (A), $\sqrt{784 + y^2} = (400 - 3y)/5$, whence $y = 45$, making $x = 197$.

So the lengths of the wires were 197 and 53 feet.

27. JUST JUNK

Say the number was N, with digits $1x1y1z1$ in that order.
Then $N \equiv -1(\text{mod } 7) \equiv -1(\text{mod } 11) \equiv -1(\text{mod } 13)$,
   so $N \equiv -1(\text{mod } 1001)$.
$N = 100000x + 1000y + 10z + 1010101$,
   so $100000x + 1000y + 10z \equiv -1010102 \equiv 908(\text{mod } 1001)$,
   whence $10(10000x + 100y + z) = 1001k + 908$, say.
That requires $k = 10t + 2$, say.
Thence, $10000x + 100y + z = 1001t + 291$.
Then dividing through by 100, and since t is obviously less than 100, we must have $t = z + 9$.
Hence, $10000x + 100y + z = 1001z + 9300$,
  so $100x + y = 10z + 93$.
But $y < 10$, so the 2nd digit of $(100x + y)$ must be zero.
Hence $z = 1$, making $x = 1$, $y = 3$.
Then $N = 1113111$.

28. A SIMPLE ROUTINE

Say the number was $(1000x + y)$, where $y < 1000$, $x < 100$.
Then, $y^2 - x = 1000x + y$, whence $(2y - 1)^2 = 4004x + 1$.
So, $(2y - 1)^2 \equiv 1(\text{mod } 7) \equiv 1(\text{mod } 11) \equiv 1(\text{mod } 13)$ and is odd.
Then, $(2y - 1) \equiv \pm1(\text{mod } 14) \equiv \pm1(\text{mod } 13) \equiv \pm1(\text{mod } 11)$.

Say $(2y - 1) = 14u + a = 13v + b$, which entails
$u = 13k - a + b$, making $(2y - 1) = 182k - 13a + 14b$
$\equiv \pm 1$ or $\pm 27 \pmod{182}$.

Then say $(2y - 1) = 182m + c = 11n + d$, which entails m
$= 11t - 2c + 2d$, where $c = \pm 1$ or ± 27 and $d = \pm 1$.

That makes $(2y - 1) = 2002t - 363c + 364d$,
whence $(2y - 1) \equiv \pm 1$, or ± 155, or ± 573, or ± 727 (mod 2002).

But $(2y - 1)^2 < 4004x + 2$, so $(2y - 1)^2 < 396398$,
making $(2y - 1) < 631$.

So there remain 3 possibilities:

$$(2y - 1) = 1 \quad 155 \quad 573$$
$$\text{making } y = 1 \quad 78 \quad 287$$
$$\text{with } x = 0 \quad 6 \quad 82$$

We may disregard the first pair of values, so leaving the two numbers 6078 and 82287.

Uncle Fred's number was 82287.

29. COMMEMORATION STAMPS

x sets: 3 at 4¢, 2 at 5¢, 5 at 10¢.
y sets: 7 at 4¢, 3 at 5¢, 3 at 10¢.
z sets: 1 at 4¢, 5 at 5¢, 4 at 10¢.

Say there were w stamps of each denomination.

Then, $3x + 7y + z = w$, $2x + 3y + 5z = w$, $5x + 3y + 4z = w$, whence $z = 3x$.

So, $4y = 12x - x = 11x$, hence $y = 11k$, say, and $x = 4k$, making $z = 12k$.

Total sets remaining would be $27k$; so, since "about 50" sets remained, $k = 2$.

Then $x = 8$, $y = 22$, $z = 24$, and $w = 202$.

So 606 stamps remained.

30. ALMOST NEIGHBORS

Say Ken's number was x.

Sum of numbers 1 to 73 $= 74 \cdot 73/2 = 2701$.

Sum of numbers $(x + 1)$ to $(x + 73) = 73x + 2701$.

Sum of numbers 1 to $(x + 73) = (x + 73)(x + 74)/2$.

So, $73x + 5402 = (x^2 + 147x + 5402)/4$,
   whence $x^2 - 145x - 16206 = 0$, so $x = 219$.
Ken's number was 219.

31. REAL ESTATE

Area of any triangle is $\sqrt{s(s - a)(s - b)(s - c)}$, where the
   sides are a, b, c, and $2s = a + b + c$.
Say sides $(x - 7)$, x, $(x + 7)$ yards, making $s = 3x/2$, and
   area $= x\sqrt{3(x^2 - 196)}/4$.

For integral values we must have $3(x^2 - 196)$ a perfect
   square, so say $x^2 - 3y^2 = 196 = 2^2 \cdot 7^2$, area $= 3xy/4$.
Neither $A^2 - 3B^2 = -7$, nor $A^2 - 3B^2 = 7$, can have an
   integral solution, so say $x = 14X$, $y = 14Y$,
   making $X^2 - 3Y^2 = 1$.
Tabulate for successive X, Y values (both X and Y conform
   to the relation $U_{n + 2} = 4U_{n + 1} - U_n$, i.e., $26 = 4 \cdot 7 - 2$):

$X =$	1	2	7	26	etc.
$Y =$	0	1	4	15	etc.
$x =$	14	28	98	364	etc.
$y =$	0	14	56	210	etc.
$3xy/4 =$	0	294	4116	57330	etc.

But 12 acres is 58080 square yards, so the area must have
   been 57330 square yards, with sides 357, 364 and 371
   yards.

32. GREETINGS

Ages: Uncle Tom X; Mark and Judy, $(Y + 1)$ and Y.
Then, $(Y + 1)^3 - Y^3 = X^2 + 1$, so $3Y^2 + 3Y = X^2$.
Say $X = 3Z$.
Then, $(2Y + 1)^2 - 3(2Z)^2 = 1$, with successive solutions:

$$2Y + 1 = 1 \quad 7 \quad 97 \quad \text{etc.}$$
$$Z = 0 \quad 2 \quad 28 \quad \text{etc.}$$

   NOTE: Both $(2Y + 1)$ and Z obey the relation
      $U_{n+2} = 14U_{n+1} - U_n$.
Here we must obviously have $Z = 28$, making $X = 84$ with
   $Y = 48$.
Uncle Tom was 84 years old.

33. AWAY FROM IT ALL

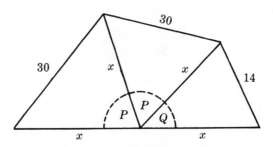

$2P + Q = 180°$, so $\cos Q = -\cos 2P = 1 - 2\cos^2 P$.
But we have $\cos P = (2x^2 - 900)/2x^2 = (x^2 - 450)/x^2$
    and $\cos Q = (2x^2 - 196)/2x^2 = (x^2 - 98)/x^2$.
Thence, $x^4 - 949x^2 + 202500 = 0$, so $x^2 = 324$ or 625. We require positive values, so $x = 18$ or 25.
But, with $x = 18$ we would have the angle P greater than 90°, making $2P > 180°$, which is not acceptable since the roads to Carlow and Lawanda both led off on the same side of the Brill/Sefton road.
Hence we must have $x = 25$, making the four villages all 25 kilometers from Mike's gates.

34. DOUBLE THE ODDS

Say there were x green marbles, y red.
After 2 greens had been drawn the chance of drawing a third green was $(x - 2)/(x + y - 2)$, with odds y to $(x - 2)$ against the event. The odds against drawing a red initially had been x to y against.

Hence $y/(x - 2) = 2x/y$, whence $2x^2 - 4x = y^2$.
Setting $y = 2z$, that becomes $(x - 1)^2 - 2z^2 = 1$.

All integral solutions may be tabulated as:

	$(x - 1) =$	1	3	17	99	etc.
with	$z =$	0	2	12	70	etc.
making	$x =$	2	4	18	100	etc.
with	$y =$	0	4	24	140	etc.

There were "about forty," so Jim had 18 green and 24 red marbles.

35. BOUNTY HUNTERS

Say x boys killed y each, $(50 - x)$ girls killed z each.
Then $25y - z(50 - x) = 19$, and $25z - xy = 11$.
Eliminating z, $625y - (xy + 11)(50 - x) = 475$,
  so $yx^2 - (50y - 11)x + 625y - 1025 = 0$.

Thence, $2yx = (50y - 11) \pm \sqrt{(3000y + 121)}$.
Say $3000y + 121 = k^2$, which has the general integral
  solution $k \equiv \pm 11$ or ± 239 (mod 750).

Hence,	$k =$ 11	239	511	etc.
with	$y =$ 0	19	87	etc.
making	$x =$ -	31	22	etc.

But, at most, xy is "around 1000."
Hence we must have $x = 31$, with $y = 19$, $z = 24$.
There were 19 girls, who killed 24 each; and 31 boys who
killed 19 each.

36. THE MURAL

We have, say: $xy = 2(w + z)$, and $wz = 2(x + y)$ where x,
y, z, w are integers. And we may assume $x \geq y$, with
$x \geq w$, $y \geq w$, $z \geq w$ (i.e., none of x, y, z is less than w).
Combining the equations, $(x - 2)(y - 2) + (z - 2)(w - 2)$
$= 8$, so we must have $w < 5$.
We can also combine the equations to give $xyw - 4x - 4y$
$= 2w^2$, whence $(wx - 4)(wy - 4) = 2w^3 + 16$.
Say $w = 1$. Then, $(x - 4)(y - 4) = 18 = 18 \cdot 1, 9 \cdot 2$,
  or $6 \cdot 3$;

whence $x =$	22 or	13 or	10
with $y =$	5	6	7
and $z =$	54	38	34.
Similarly, if $w = 2$, $x =$	10 or	6	
with $y =$	3	4	
and $z =$	13	10.	
If $w = 3$, $x =$	13 or	6	
with $y =$	2	3	
and $z =$	10	6.	
If $w = 4$, $x =$	10 or	4	
with $y =$	2	4	
and $z =$	6	4.	

Hence we have 7 different pairs:
  54 by 1, 22 by 5; 38 by 1, 13 by 6; 34 by 1, 10 by 7;
  13 by 2, 10 by 3; 10 by 2, 6 by 4; 6 by 3, 6 by 3;
   4 by 4,   4 by 4.

37. A WOMAN'S JOB

Say Bill could do $1/x$ of the job per minute, Ann $1/12y$ of the job. To do the lot alone Ann would take $12y$ minutes. So Bill worked alone for $5y$ minutes, leaving $(x - 5y)/x$ for Ann to do.

To do that, Ann took $12y(x - 5y)/x$ minutes.

Together they would have taken $12xy/(x + 12y)$ minutes to do the lot, in which time Bill alone would have done $12y/(x + 12y)$ of the job.

So, $12y/(x + 12y) = (x - 5y)/2x$, whence $x = 20y$.

In fact, they took $5y + 12y(x - 5y)/x$ minutes, i.e., $7x/10$ minutes.

Together they would have taken $12xy/(x + 12y)$, i.e., $3x/8$ minutes.

So, $7x/10 - 3x/8 = 52$, whence $x = 160$, with $y = 8$.

Their total time was 1 hour and 52 minutes.

38. EACH TO EACH

Say the numbers of people involved in the exchange of cards for the three successive years were z, y, x, where $x > y > z$.

Corresponding numbers of cards:
  $x(x - 1), y(y - 1), z(z - 1)$.

So, $(x^2 - x) - (y^2 - y) = 84$,
  i.e., $(2x - 1)^2 - (2y - 1)^2 = 4 \cdot 84 = 4 \cdot 2^2 \cdot 3 \cdot 7$.

Tablulate for factors:

$[(2x - 1) + (2y - 1)]/2$ =	84	42	28	21	14	12
$[(2x - 1) - (2y - 1)]/2$ =	1	2	3	4	6	7
$(2x - 1)$ =	85	44	31	25	20	19
$(2y - 1)$ =	83	40	25	17	8	5
x =	43	—	16	13	—	10
y =	42	—	13	9	—	3

Similarly we get "possibles" for y and z as:
  $y = 43$ 16   13   10
  $z = 42$ 13   9   3

But the value of y must be the same in each case.
So, $x = 16$, $y = 13$, $z = 9$.
That last Xmas $16(16 - 1)$, i.e., 240, cards were exchanged.

39. THE JEWEL BOX

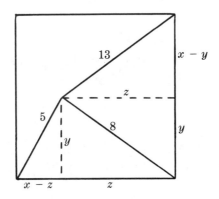

$y^2 = 5^2 - (x - z)^2 = 8^2 - z^2$, so $z = (x^2 + 39)/2x$.
$z^2 = 8^2 - y^2 = 13^2 - (x - y)^2$, so $y = (x^2 - 105)/2x$.
Then, $y^2 = (x^2 - 105)^2/4x^2$.
But, $y^2 = 64 - z^2$, so $y^2 = 64 - (x^2 + 39)^2/4x^2$,
   hence, $(x^2 - 105)^2 = 256x^2 - (x^2 + 39)^2$,
   whence $x^4 - 194x^2 + 6273 = 0$, with solution $x^2 = 41$ or
   153.
But, from the expression for y, $x^2 > 105$. Hence we must
   have $x^2 = 153$.
So the top of the box had area 153 square cm.

40. PETER'S PENNIES

Say Peter had m^2 pennies.
Totals for hexagon formation are successively 1, 7, 19, 37,
   etc., from which we see that the total $m^2 = 3n^2 - 3n + $
   1, corresponding to n pennies per side in the hexagon,
   m and n being whole numbers.
Then, $6n = 3 \pm \sqrt{3(4m^2 - 1)}$.
For integral values $4m^2 - 1 = 3k^2$, say.
Hence, $(2m)^2 - 3k^2 = 1$.

Successive values in this equation are:
$$m = 1 \quad 13 \quad 181 \quad \text{etc.},$$
$$k = 1 \quad 15 \quad 209 \quad \text{etc.},$$
both m and k obeying the rule $U_r = 14U_{r-1} - U_{r-2}$.
But $13^2 = 169$, and $181^2 = 32761$, so obviously Peter had 169 pennies on the table. Then 32761 pennies would be required for the next bigger case, so that would entail 32592 more.

41. SO VERY SIMPLE

The number was x, with $(n - 1)$ digits, special digit y.
Then $29x = 10x + (10^n + 1)y$, whence $(10^n - 1)y = 19x$, so $10^n \equiv -1 \pmod{19}$.
All to (mod 19): $10^2 \equiv 5$, $10^3 \equiv -7$, $10^4 \equiv 6$, $10^5 \equiv 3$, $10^6 \equiv -8$, $10^7 \equiv -4$, $10^8 \equiv -2$, $10^9 \equiv -1$.

So we have $n = 9$, hence x has 8 digits.
Then $19x = 1000000001y$, $x = 52631579y$.
But our x has 8 digits, so $y = 1$, $x = 52631579$.
Mike's number was 52631579, his "special digit" was 1.

42. POWER PLAY

Say $x^2 = 2y^3 = 3z^5 = 2^{2a} \cdot 3^{2b}$, hence $x = 2^a \cdot 3^b$.
Then, $y^3 = 2^{(2a-1)} \cdot 3^{2b}$, so $2a - 1 = 3u$, say,
  whence $a = 3m - 1$, $b = 3n$, say,
  making $y^3 = 2^{(6m-3)} \cdot 3^{6n}$, hence $y = 2^{(2m-1)} \cdot 3^{2n}$.
Then $x^2 = 2^{(6m-2)} \cdot 3^{6n} = 3z^5$,
  so $z^5 = 2^{(6m-2)} \cdot 3^{(6n-1)}$, hence $m = 5k + 2$, $n = 5t + 1$.
Then we have $z = 2^{(6k+2)} \cdot 3^{(6t+1)}$,
  with $x = 2^{(15k+5)} \cdot 3^{(15t+3)}$,
  and $y = 2^{(10k+3)} \cdot 3^{(10t+2)}$.
For minimal positive values $k = t = 0$, making
  $x = 2^5 \cdot 3^3 = 864$, $y = 2^3 \cdot 3^2 = 72$, $z = 2^2 \cdot 3 = 12$.

The next greater values entail $k = 1$, $t = 0$, making
  $x = 2^{20} \cdot 3^3$, obviously unacceptable as a house number.
So the numbers were: Bruce 864, Jane 72, Tom 12.

43. THE COLLECTOR

$59x + 199y + 287z + 344(100 - x - y - z) = 10000$,
  whence $285x + 145y + 57z = 24400$,
  so $57(5x + z) + 145y = 24400$.

Then, since x, y, z are integers, $(24400 - 145y)$ must be
  divisible by 57, hence $y = 57k + 13$ with k any integer.
Now, $y < 10000/199$, so $y < 51$. Hence we must have
  $k = 0$, with $y = 13$.
Then $5x + z = 395$, so $x + z = 395 - 4x$.
But $(x + z) < 87$, so $4x > 308$, whence $x > 77$.
Also, re $(5x + z)$, $x < 79$. So $x = 78$, making $z = 5$.
Hence Walt bought: 78 at \$0.59, 13 at \$1.99, 5 at \$2.87, 4
  at \$3.44.

44. A MATTER OF SQUARES

Say the number had digits x, y, z in that order.
Then, $x^2 + y^2 + z^2 = (100x + 10y + z)/2$, so z must be even.
Say $z = 2w$, making $x^2 + y^2 + 4w^2 = 50x + 5y + w$,
  whence $(50 - 2x)^2 + (2y - 5)^2 = 2525 - 4w(4w - 1)$, with
  $w < 5$.
Set $X = 50 - 2x$ and $Y = 2y - 5$, where $X < 50$, $Y \le 13$.

Now consider the possible values for w. Note that if $N =
kt^2$, k being *quadratfrei* (i.e., no square factor), then N
cannot be the sum of two integral squares if k has any
factor of the form $(4n - 1)$.

$w = 0$, $X^2 + Y^2 = 2525 = 50^2 + 5^2 = 34^2 + 37^2 = 26^2 + 43^2$,
  all being unacceptable.
$w = 1$, $X^2 + Y^2 = 2513 = 359 \cdot 7$, impossible re 7.
$w = 2$, $X^2 + Y^2 = 2469 = 823 \cdot 3$, impossible re 3.
$w = 3$, $X^2 + Y^2 = 2393 = 32^2 + 37^2$, unacceptable.
$w = 4$, $X^2 + Y^2 = 2285 = 457 \cdot 5 = (21^2 + 4^2)(2^2 + 1^2)$
  $= 38^2 + 29^2 = 46^2 + 13^2$.
But $Y \le 13$, so we must have $X = 46$, $Y = 13$.

Thence $x = 2$, $y = 9$, $z = 8$, making the number 298.

45. THE ONLY TREE

House number $2n$, the even numbers going up to $2m$.
Then sum of even numbers above Steve's was:
$$[m(m + 1) - n(n + 1)],$$
  and sum of even numbers below his was: $n(n - 1)$.
So $m(m + 1) - n(n + 1) = n(n - 1)/2$.
  Whence $(6n + 1)^2 - 6(2m + 1)^2 = -5$ (A)

Now, $1^2 - 6 \cdot 1^2 = -5$, so all integral solutions of (A) are given by: $6n + 1 = \pm(a \pm 6b)$, $2m + 1 = \pm(a \pm b)$, the "internal" + and − signs in agreement,
where $a^2 - 6b^2 = 1$.   (B)

The two smallest integral solutions of (B) are:
$$(a, b) = (1, 0) \text{ and } (5, 2),$$
so all further successive (a, b) pairs are given by:
$$a_{r+2} = 10a_{r+1} - a_r, \ b_{r-2} = 10b_{r+1} - b_r.$$

We now tabulate for successive (a, b) pairs, observing that we require $n < 50$:

$a =$	1	5	5	49	49	485	etc.
$b =$	0	2	2	20	20	198	etc.
$6n + 1 =$	1	7	17	71	169	703	etc.
$2m + 1 =$	1	3	7	29	69	287	etc.
$n =$	0	1	—	—	28	117	etc.
$m =$	0	1	—	—	34	143	etc.

So there were 34 even numbers, Steve's being 56.

46. IT MAKES SENSE

Here we have calculations using a scale of notation that is not our usual denary scale. In solving the problem it is convenient to use the denary scale, however.

Say the calculations were in scale-n notation, i.e., to base n.
Then we have $(n^2 + 2n + 1) + (2n^2 + n + 2) = 43 \cdot 3$,
so $n^2 + n - 42 = 0$, whence $n = 6$.
Hence 111 means $(36 + 6 + 1)$, i.e., 43 in scale 10,
and 11 means $(6 + 1)$, i.e., 7 in scale-10.

So we have the required total as 93 in scale-10 notation.
But $93 = 2 \cdot 6^2 + 3 \cdot 6 + 3$, which in scale-6 notation would be written as 233.
Hence we would answer the question in words as: "two three three." Of course denary scale words, such as twenty, hundred, etc., cannot be used when working in a non-denary scale notation.

47. GRANDPA'S BIRTHDAY

Ages: Doug, x years; grandfather, $(10y + z)$ years.
Then, $x(x + 1)/2 = 10y + z + 1$, and $x = y + z$.

Thence, $x^2 - x = 18y + 2$, so $(2x - 1)^2 = 72y + 9$.
Say $(2x - 1) = 3k$, making $k^2 = 8y + 1$, with $y < 10$.
Tabulate:

	$k^2 =$	9	25	49
	$2x - 1 =$	9	15	21
	$x =$	5	8	11
	$y =$	1	3	6
	$z =$	4	5	5
Grandfather		14	35	65
Doug		5	8	11

Obviously the ages were 65 and 11 years.

48. VANDALISM

List the Lowest Common Multiples of the possible sets of
correct fraction denominators:

4, 5, 7, 9—L.C.M. 1260   3, 5, 7, 9—L.C.M. 315
3, 4, 7, 9—L.C.M. 252   3, 4, 5, 9—L.C.M. 180
3, 4, 5, 7—L.C.M. 420

But there were only 300 birds originally, so the number
  remaining must have been 252 or 180. And the incorrect
  fraction must have been 1/5 or 1/7.
But more than 100 birds escaped, so 180 must have remained, the fraction 1/7 being incorrect.
Then there remained: 60 finches
                      45 budgies
                      36 canaries
                      20 parrots
                      and 19 mynah birds and others.
Now, the original number of canaries was equal to three
  times the number of parrots remaining, so there had
  been 60 canaries, of which 24 canaries escaped.

49. TRANSPORTATION

Say 3 groups A, B, C of 10 each, starting time zero.
(1) Truck takes A a distance of x miles, taking $x/40$ hours.
(2) Meanwhile B and C walk $x/10$ miles, so B and C are
    $9x/10$ miles behind A when truck drops group A.
(3) Truck drives back, picks up B and transports to join

group A that has continued on foot, and drives back again. Truck picks up group C and transports right to Tulla to arrive there at the same time as A and B.

(4) So truck makes 4 trips after dropping group A:
to "close" $9x/10$ miles at 34 miles per hour, $9x/340$ hours;
to overtake $9x/10$ miles at 36 m.p.h., $9x/360$ hours;
to "close" $9x/10$ miles at 34 m.p.h., $9x340$ hours;
to overtake $9x/10$ miles at 36 m.p.h., $9x/360$ hours.
Those 4 trips take total of $7x/68$ hours.

(5) But, while the truck does those 4 trips, group A walks final $(24 - x)$ miles at 4 m.p.h., taking $(24 - x)/4$ hours. Hence $7x/68 = (24 - x)/4$, whence $x = 17$.

So total time for the complete operation is $(17/40 + 7/4)$, i.e., $87/40$ hours: 2 hours, $10\frac{1}{2}$ minutes.

50. JUST FOR FUN

$N = 10000x + y = y^2/2 - x$, whence $y^2 - 2y = 20002x$, so $(y - 1)^2 = 20002x + 1$.

Hence, $(y - 1) \equiv \pm1(\mod 274) \equiv \pm1(\mod 73)$.
Say $(y - 1) = 274u + a = 73v + b$,
   entailing $u = 73k - 4a + 4b$, say.
Then $(y - 1) = 20002k - 1095a + 1096b$,
   where $a = \pm1$, $b = \pm1$.
Thence $(y - 1) \equiv \pm1$ or $\pm2191 \ (\mod 20002)$.
But $(y - 1) < 9999$, so $(y - 1) = 1$ or 2191.
With $(y - 1) = 1$, we have $x = 0$, obviously unacceptable.
Hence $(y - 1) = 2191$, making $x = 240$, $y = 2192$.

The complete number was 240-2192.

51. GOOD SERVICE

Poole trains leave at intervals of x minutes, Tulla trains at intervals of y minutes; x and y being integers.
Counting in minutes from 6:00 a.m., $18x = 17y + 5$, whence $x = 17k + 5$, $y = 18k + 5$.

But, in approximately 19 hours, between say 1080 and 1140 minutes from 6:00 a.m., departures coincide only twice, so that $xy > 25$, and also $xy < 1599$ (i.e., $39 \cdot 41$).

So we must have $k = 1$, making $x = 22$, $y = 23$.
Hence the first coincidence is at 12:36 p.m. (shortly after noon).
The intervals being 22 and 23 minutes, the next coincidence occurs 506 minutes later, which is at 9:02 p.m.

52. BOTH HANDS

Say time "is": x hours, y minutes, with hour hand at the $(60x + y)/12$ minute division, and the minute hand at the y minutes division.

Earlier that day the time had been z hours, w minutes, with hour hand at the $(60z + w)/12$ minute division, and the minute hand at the w minutes division.

Then, $(60z + w)/12 = y$, and $w = (60x + y)/12 - 1$,
  whence $720z + 60x - 143y = 12$.
All of x, y, z, w are integers, so that entails $y = 12k$.

Then, $60z + 5x - 143k = 1$, hence $k = 5t - 2$.
But $y < 60$, so $k < 5$, hence we require $k = 3$, making $y = 36$.
Thence $5x = 430 - 60z$, so $x = 86 - 12z$.
But $x < 12$, so we must have $z = 7$, with $x = 2$.
We had $w = (60x + y)/12 - 1$, so $w = 12$.

When Joe asked, the time was 2:36 p.m.; when Ben checked his watch earlier that day the time had been 7:12 a.m.

53. LONG ODDS

Odds of 11 to 2 against implies a chance of 2/13.
Say Pat picked up $(y + 1)$ cards, $(x + 1)$ being spades.
Then, $\dfrac{(x + 1)x(x - 1)}{(y + 1)y(y - 1)} = \dfrac{2}{13}$, hence $13x(x^2 - 1) = 2y(y^2 - 1)$.
But $(x + 1) < 14$, so $2y(y^2 - 1) < 169 \cdot 168$, $y(y^2 - 1) < 14196$.
But $25(25^2 - 1) = 15600$, so $y < 25$.

Now, y or $(y - 1)$ or $(y + 1)$ must be a multiple of 13, hence $y = 12$ or 13 or 14.

Substituting for y, neither $y = 12$ nor $y = 14$ gives an integral value for x. But with $y = 13$, we have $x = 7$.

So Pat picked up 14 cards, including 8 spades.

54. THE TALKATIVE GUEST

Remember the old chestnut in logic. It is true that "All men with red hair are males," but surely not true that "All males are men with red hair"!

List the various statements:
  (1) Doug dentist if Ben banker.
  (2) Doug actor if Andy curate.
  (3) Ben actor ONLY if Doug dentist.
  (4) Ben banker if Clem actor.
  (5) Doug curate UNLESS Clem dentist OR Ben banker.

Ben is not the curate. If he is the banker, Doug must be the dentist (1), which makes Ben the actor (3).
If Ben is the actor, Doug must be the dentist (3). Then, re (2), Andy is not the curate. So Andy would be the banker and Clem the curate: impossible re (5).
So Ben is the dentist, with Doug the curate (5). Then, re (4), Clem is not the actor; so Clem must be the banker and Andy the actor.

Andy was the actor, Ben the dentist, Clem the banker, Doug the curate.

55. URANIUM TRIANGLES

Say sides were 17, 28, x feet and 17, 28, y feet.
Any triangle with sides a, b, c has area
$\sqrt{s(s - a)(s - b)(s - c)}$, where $a + b + c = 2s$.
So, using the formula and squaring, we get:
$$(45^2 - x^2)(x^2 - 11^2) = (45^2 - y^2)(y^2 - 11^2).$$
Then, setting $X = x^2$, $Y = y^2$, and simplifying, $(X - 1073)^2 = (Y - 1073)^2$.
But we require x and y to be different, hence we must have $(X - 1073) = -(Y - 1073)$, whence $X + Y = 2146$.
So, $x^2 + y^2 = 2146 = 11^2 + 45^2 = 25^2 + 39^2$.
But (28, 17, 11) and (28, 17, 45) cannot be sides of triangles.
Hence the respective third sides were 25 and 39 feet.

56. MEN ON THE MOON

Say caches were set up at points A, B, C distant from starting point, at a miles, $(a + b)$ miles, and $(a + b + c)$ miles respectively. We call a unit of fuel a fuel-mile, and the crawler carries 315 such units.

(1) 3 round-trip runs to A, each time leaving $(x - 2a)$ units.
   1 one-way run to A, arriving with spare $(x - a)$ units.
   Then at A there will be available $(4x - 7a)$ units.
(2) 2 round-trip runs to B, each time leaving $(x - 2b)$ units.
   1 one-way run to B, arriving with spare $(x - b)$ units.
   Then at B there will be available $(3x - 5b)$ units.
   Fuel expended, A to B, totals $5b$ units.
   So, $4x - 7a = 3x - 5b + 5b$, whence $x = 7a$.
(3) 1 round-trip run to C, leaving $(x - 2c)$ units.
   1 one-way run to C, arriving with spare $(x - c)$ units.
   Then at C there will be available $(2x - 3c)$ units.
   Fuel expended, B to C, totals $3c$ units.
   So, $3x - 5b = 2x - 3c + 3c$, whence $x = 5b$.
(4) 1 final one-way run, using x units.
   Then $2x - 3c = x$, whence $x = 3c$.

But $x = 315$, so $a = 45$, $b = 63$, $c = 105$. So caches were set up at 45, 108 and 213 miles from the starting point. All runs were made fully laden with fuel as shown in the detailed analysis. Total distance traveled by the crawler was 1260 miles.

57. A FRIENDLY TELLER

Check: $(10x + y)$ dollars, $(10z + w)$ cents.
Payment: $(10w + z)$ dollars, $(10y + x)$ cents.
So $2000x + 200y + 20z + 2w = 1000w + 100z + 10y + x + 125$, whence $1999x + 190y - 80z - 998w = 125$.
Obviously, w must be twice or three times x, so $x < 5$.
Also, from the equation, x must be odd.

Say $x = 3$. Then $40z - 95y + 499w = 2936$, entailing $w = 9$.
   But that leads to $19y - 8z = 311$, which is impossible since $y < 10$.

Say $x = 1$. Then $40z - 95y + 499w = 937$, entailing $w = 3$. Thence, $19y - 8z = 112$, so $y = 8$, $z = 5$.

So the check was for \$18.53, the payment \$35.81.

58. MANY A MICKLE

Say there were $(n + 1)$ amounts listed, and that each charity would receive $m¢$.
Then, $24 + 122(1 + 2 + 4 + \ldots + 2^{n-1}) - 5200 = 11m$, so $122 \cdot 2^n = 11m + 5298$, whence $61 \cdot 2^n \equiv 9 \pmod{11}$, which entails $2^n \equiv -4 \pmod{11}$.

Now, all to $\pmod{11}$ we have $2^2 \equiv 4$, and $2^5 \equiv -1$,
  so $2^7 \equiv -4$, and $2^7 \equiv 2^{17} \equiv 2^{27}$, etc.
Hence $n = 7$, or 17, or 27, etc.
With $n = 7$, we have $m = 938$, and with $n = 27$, $m > 10^9$.
Obviously each charity would receive more than \$9.38, so we must have $n = 17$, with $m = 1453226$.

So each charity would receive \$14,532.26.

59. A TALE OF WOE

Take the second day as No. 1, sales the first day being $x¢$.
Then on successive days sales in cents were: No. 0: x, No. 1: $(2x + 3)/3$, No. 2: $(4x + 24)/9$, No. 3: $(8x + 129)/27$, No. 4: $(16x + 582)/81$, etc.

So sales for day number n were $(2^n x + 3U_n)/3^n$, where $U_1 = 1$, $U_2 = 8$, $U_3 = 43$, $U_4 = 194$, and $U_n = 2U_{n-1} + 3^{n-1}n$.
Say $U_n = n \cdot 3^n A + n \cdot 2^n B + 3^n C + 2^n D + E$. Obviously $U_0 = 0$. Then, substituting our known numerical values of U_n for $n = 0, 1, 2, 3, 4$ we have a system of 5 linear equations. Solving that system we find:
$$A = 1, B = 0, C = -2, D = 2, E = 0.$$
Hence $U_n = 3^n \cdot n - 2 \cdot 3^n + 2 \cdot 2^n = 3^n(n - 2) + 2^{n+1}$.

So sales for day number n were:
  $2^n(x + 6)/3^n + 3n - 6$, which equaled 533 cents.
Hence, $2^n(x + 6)/3^n + 3n = 539$.
Then $(x + 6)$ must be divisible by 3^n, so $(x + 6) = 3^n k$, where k is an integer, whence $2^n k = 539 - 3n$.

From the wording, $n > 3$. Also, since $2^{10} = 1024$, $n < 10$.
And $(539 - 3n)$ must be even, so n must be odd.
Testing for $n = 5, 7$, and 9 we have integral k only with
  $n = 9$, $k = 1$. Hence $x = 19677$.
The first day sales amounted to \$196.77, and they were in
  business for 10 working days.

60. QUITE A FAMILY

Say ages were: boys $(x - 2)$, x, $(x + 2)$ years;
          girls $(y - 1)$, $(y + 1)$ years.
Then $x^2 - 2y^2 = -2$.
Say $x = 2z$, whence $y^2 - 2z^2 = 1$.
Tabulate solutions: $y = 1$ 3 17 etc.
                      $z = 0$ 2 12 etc.
                      $x = 0$ 4 24 etc.,
x, y, z all obeying relation $U_{n+2} = 6U_{n+1} - U_n$.

No further solutions could yield acceptable ages, and
  John said the ages were all different. Hence we must
  have $x = 24$, $y = 17$, making the ages: boys 22, 24, 26
  years, and girls 16, 18 years.

61. NUMBERS, NUMBERS

Say the two "halves" were X and Y, each < 1000.
Then, $X^2 + Y^2 + 1 = 1000X + Y$,
  so $(2X - 1000)^2 + (2Y - 1)^2 = 999997 = 1321 \cdot 757$.
$1321 \cdot 757 = (36^2 + 5^2)(26^2 + 9^2)$
         $= (36 \cdot 26 \pm 9 \cdot 5)^2 + (36 \cdot 9 \mp 26 \cdot 5)^2$
         $= (891^2 + 454^2)$ or $(981^2 + 194^2)$.

Tabulate:

$2X - 1000 =$	-454	$+454$	-194	$+194$
$2Y - 1 =$	891	891	981	981
$X =$	273	727	403	597
$Y =$	446	446	491	491

So there were 3 other 6-digit numbers that met the requirements: 273446, 597491 and 727446.

62. THE YEARS THAT COUNT

Ages: Sam x; boys, y and 9; wife, z years.

Then, $\dfrac{x^2 + y^2 + 9^2}{x + y + 9} = z$, and $(x + y + 9)$ is a factor of $(x^2 + y^2 + 9^2)$.

That entails general solution:
$$x = a(a + b + c)$$
$$y = b(a + b + c)$$
$$9 = c(a + b + c)$$
$$\text{with } z = a^2 + b^2 + c^2$$

a, b, c being integers.

From $c(a + b + c)$ we have $c = 9$, or 3, or 1.

With $c = 9$ or with $c = 3$, we would have negative values for a and b.

So, $c = 1$, whence $a + b = 8$. Then, taking $a > b$, and since obviously $y > 9$ and $z > (y + 10)$ say, we must have:
$$a = 6, \ b = 2, \ x = 54, \ y = 18, \ z = 41.$$

Sam was 54 years old, his wife 41, the boys 18 and 9.

63. A FUNNY FRACTION

Say the amount was x dollars and y cents.

Then $10^n y + x = (500x + 5y)/8$, where x has n digits.

Hence $y(8 \cdot 10^n - 5) = 492x$.

Now set $x = 5w$, $y = 4z$, whence $z(16 \cdot 10^{n-1} - 1) = 123w$.

But $(16 \cdot 10^{n-1} - 1)$ is a multiple of 3 for all n,
so $(16 \cdot 10^{n-1} - 1) = 3k$, whence $zk = 41w$.

Then, since $y < 100$, we have $z < 25$, so k must be a multiple of 41, whence $16 \cdot 10^{n-1} \equiv 1 \pmod{41}$.

Now say $16 \cdot 10^{n-1} = 41t + 1$, which entails
$$10^{n-1} = 41m + 18.$$

So $10^{n-1} \equiv 18 \pmod{41}$.

By quick trial we find the minimal solution with $n = 3$.

Thence, from our original equation, $65y = 4x$, with general solution $x = 65r$, $y = 4r$, say. The minimal value for a 3-digit x entails $r = 2$, making $x = 130$, $y = 8$.

The amount was $130.08.

64. TWO MAGIC SQUARES

Say a Magic Square has numbers $(x + 1)$ to $(x + r^2)$, where $x + r^2 = 54$.

Then it has r^2 numbers from $(55 - r^2)$ to 54 inclusive, making a gross total of $r^2(109 - r^2)/2$, a magic total of $r(109 - r^2)/2$.

Say our two Magic Squares have m^2 and n^2 numbers respectively, with $m > n$.
Then $\qquad m(109 - m^2)/2 = n(109 - n^2)/2$,
whence $\qquad m^3 - n^3 = 109(m - n)$.
Now, $m \neq n$, so we may divide through by $(m - n)$,
giving $\qquad m^2 + mn + n^2 = 109$,
whence $\quad (2m + n)^2 + 3n^2 = 109 \cdot 4$
$$= (1^2 + 3 \cdot 6^2)(1^2 + 3 \cdot 1^2),$$
with integral solutions $m = 7$, $n = 5$, or $m = 5$, $n = 7$.
But $m > n$, so we must have $m = 7$, $n = 5$.
Hence the respective Magic Squares must have numbers from 6 to 54, and 30 to 54, respectively.

65. THE JOKER'S WILD

They started with: Jack x cents, Bob y cents.
After n wins by Jack they had:
   Jack: $x + y(3^n - 2^n)/3^n$, Bob: $2^n y/3^n$.
After a further n wins by Bob:
   Jack had $2^n[x + y(3^n - 2^n)/3^n]/3^n$.
But that equaled $(x + y)/4$.

Hence, $3^n(4 \cdot 2^n - 3^n)x = [3^{2n} - 4 \cdot 2^n(3^n - 2^n)]y$,
   with solution: $x = (3^{2n} - 4 \cdot 2^n \cdot 3^n + 4 \cdot 2^{2n})k$,
$$y = 3^n(4 \cdot 2^n - 3^n)k.$$
So, $(x + y)/4 = 2^{2n}k$, where k is an integer.
Now Jack lost, so $x > (x + y)/4$.
Say $3^n = a$, and $2^n = b$. Then, $a^2 + 3b^2 > 4ab$, hence $a > 3b$.
That entails $3^n > 3 \cdot 2^n$, so $n > 2$.
But we must have $4 \cdot 2^n > 3^n$, so $n < 4$.
Hence, $n = 3$, making $x = 121k$, $y = 135k$, $(x + y) = 256k$.
Jack ended up with $64k$ so he lost $57k$ cents. But that was "almost exactly \$4," so $k = 7$.
Then $x = 847$, $y = 945$. Jack started with \$8.47, Bob with \$9.45.

66. EASY COME EASY GO

Say y pairs at \$1.35, x number of cents on the invoice.
Then, $135y = 100(x^2 + 3) + x$, whence $100x^2 + x + 300 = 135y$, and $135 = 27 \cdot 5$.

Dividing $(100x^2 + x + 300)$ by 100 we have
$(x^2 + x/100 + 3)$.

Now, $\dfrac{27 \cdot 37 + 1}{100} = 10$, so $\dfrac{1}{100} \equiv 10 \pmod{27}$.

Hence, $x^2 + 10x + 3 \equiv 0 \pmod{27}$,
    whence $(x + 5) \equiv \pm 7 \pmod{27}$.
So $(x + 5) = 27k \pm 7$, say.
But, $(x^2 + 3) < 500$, so $x < 23$.
Obviously $x \ne 2$. Hence we must have $(x + 5) = 20, x = 15$.

So the total amount was $228.15, for 169 pairs.

67. A BUG IN A BARN

It is well known that the angle of incidence equals the
angle of reflection, the path of such a ray being the
shortest possible. Hence the route of the roach would
correspond to that of a ray of light reflected by the
front and back walls. So, the diagrams depict the actual
and virtual situations, the angles at D and E all being
equal.

ACTUAL   VIRTUAL

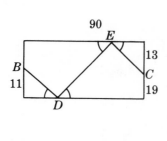

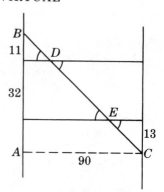

So we have $(BC)^2 = 56^2 + 90^2$, making $BC = 106$.
The shortest possible route was 106 feet.

68. WRONG NUMBER

Say Joe's number was $(100y + 10x + z)$, where x and z are
single-digit numbers, and y is an integer less than 100.

Then $1000x + 10y + z = 300y + 30x + 3z,$
    whence $5(97x - 29y) = z.$
Then we must have $z = 5$, making $97x - 29y = 1.$
That equation has general integral solution:
$$x = 29k + 3$$
$$y = 97k + 10$$
Within permissible limits, therefore, $x = 3$, $y = 10$.
So, Joe's number was 1035.

69. AT THE SHOW

Say X boys, Y girls. Then the total number of different
    arrangements in one row is $\lfloor(X + Y).$
Then the total number of different arrangements with a
    girl at each end would be $Y(Y - 1) \lfloor (X + Y - 2),$ so
    chances of a girl at each end will be:
$$\frac{Y(Y - 1) \lfloor(X + Y - 2)}{\lfloor(X + Y)}, \text{ i.e., } \frac{Y(Y - 1)}{(X + Y)(X + Y - 1)}.$$
But "2 to 1 odds against" is one chance in three,
    so $\dfrac{Y(Y - 1)}{(X + Y)(X + Y - 1)} = \dfrac{1}{3}$,
    whence $2Y^2 - 2XY - X^2 = 2Y - X.$
Setting $k = 2Y - X$, this becomes $k^2 - 2k = 3X^2,$
    whence $(k - 1)^2 - 3X^2 = 1.$
This Pellian equation has successive integral solutions
    that may be tabulated as:

$(k - 1) =$	1	2	7	26	97	etc.,
$X =$	0	1	4	15	56	etc.,
with $Y =$	1	2	6	21	77	etc.

But we require $X > 4$, re 5 Barton boys,
    and $(X + Y) < 100.$
So we must have $X = 15$, $Y = 21.$
Hence there were 36 in the group: 21 girls and 15 boys.

70. THE PENALTY CLAUSE

Say x plants, and y minutes penalty time.
Then, $37x - y(y + 1)/2 = 700,$
    whence $(2y + 1)^2 = 296x - 5599$, and $296 = 37 \cdot 8.$
Hence $(2y + 1)^2 \equiv -5599 \pmod 8 \equiv -5599 \pmod{37}$
    so $(2y + 1) \equiv \pm 1 \pmod 2 \equiv \pm 5 \pmod{37}.$

Thence, $(2y + 1) \equiv \pm5(\text{mod } 74)$.

But we have "nearly 90 of them in all," so $x < 90$, whence we must have $y(y + 1) < 5260$, entailing $y < 73$, and $(2y + 1) < 147$.

Possible values may be tabulated:

$$2y + 1 = 69 \quad 79 \quad 143$$
$$\text{making } y = 34 \quad 39 \quad 71$$
$$\text{with } x = 35 \quad 40 \quad 88$$

Then, for "nearly 90," $x = 88$, with $y = 71$.

There were 88 rose standards in all.

71. CONSECUTIVE SQUARES

Say $N = 10000y + 6789$, y being a 3-digit integer.

Then $10000y + 6789 = (x - 1)^2 + x^2 + (x + 1)^2 = 3x^2 - 2$, say.

Dividing through by 3, we see that $y = 3z - 1$, say.

So $x^2 = 10000z - 1071$, whence $x^2 \equiv -1071(\text{mod } 10000)$, giving $x^2 \equiv 1(\text{mod } 16) \equiv 179(\text{mod } 625)$.

Say $f(x) = x^2 - 179 \equiv 0(\text{mod } 5)$, making $x = 5a \pm 2$, say.

Then $f(x) = 25a^2 \pm 20a - 175 \equiv 0(\text{mod } 25)$,
   hence $5a^2 \pm 4a - 35 \equiv 0(\text{mod } 5)$, so $a = 5b$, say,
   making $x = 25b \pm 2$.

Then $f(x) = 25^2b^2 \pm 100b - 175 \equiv 0(\text{mod } 125)$,
   hence $25b^2 \pm 4b - 7 \equiv 0(\text{mod } 5)$, so $b = 5c \pm 3$,
   making $x = 125c \pm 77$.

Then $f(x) = 125^2c^2 \pm 125 \cdot 154c + 5750 \equiv 0(\text{mod } 625)$,
   hence $125c^2 \pm 154c + 46 \equiv 0(\text{mod } 5)$, so $c = 5d \pm 1$,
   making $x = 625d \pm 202$.

So we have $x \equiv \pm202(\text{mod } 625) \equiv \pm1(\text{mod } 8)$, which entails $x \equiv \pm423$ or $\pm1673(\text{mod } 5000)$.

Hence, since we require $3x^2 < 9999999$, $x = 423$ or 1673.

But with $x = 423$ we have $N = 536789$, a 6-digit number.

Hence we must have $x = 1673$, making $N = 8396789$.

72. THINK OF A NUMBER

Say the overall area of the square patio was x^2 square feet, the internal rectangular lawn having an area of 414 square feet.

Then $x^2 - 414 = 7y$, whence $x^2 \equiv 1(\text{mod } 7)$.

So $x \equiv \pm1(\text{mod } 7)$.

Now, $x^2 - 414 < 414$, whence $x < 29$.

Also, the longer side of the internal lawn is 23 feet, so $x > 23$.

Hence we must have $x = 27$, making the paved area 315. So Fran's key number was 45.

73. A DEAL IN STAMPS

Say, x stamps at x cents, y stamps at $5y$ cents.

Then, $x^2 - 5y^2 = 319$, and $x^2 + 5y^2 =$ about 3200.

Now, $319 = 29 \cdot 11$, so the equation can be solved analytically, there being two families of integral pairs of (x, y) values. But here it seems that inspired trial is justified.

Adding the two equations, $2x^2 =$ about 3519, so we must have $x =$ about 42.

Obviously, from the first equation, x^2 ends with 4 or 9, so we need test only $x = 38, 42, 43,$ and 47:

$x =$	38	42	43	47
$x^2 =$	1444	1764	1849	2209
making $5y^2 =$	1125	1445	1530	1890
$y^2 =$	225	289	306	378
integral $y =$	15	17	—	—
$x^2 + 5y^2 =$	2569	3209		

We may reject the first case, since all requirements are obviously met by the results in the second.

Hence, he bought 42 stamps at 42¢ average, and 17 at 85¢ average, for a total of $32.09.

74. A SERIAL NUMBER

Say the serial number $N = (10000001x + 10y)$, where $y < 10^6$.

Then $N = (11x)^5$, so y is a multiple of 11 and of x.

Say $y = 11xz$, whence $14641x^4 = 10z + 909091$.

Now since $x^4 > 909091/14641$, $x > 2$.

$11xz < 1000000$, so $xz < 90909$, and $x \geq 3$,

so $z < 30303$, whence $14641x^4 < (303030 + 909091)$.

Hence $x^4 < 83$, so $x < 4$.

But, $x \geq 3$. Hence $x = 3$, making $z = 27683$, $y = 913539$.

The serial number was 39135393.

75. AN EVENING OUT

Stan started with: x dollars in bills, $2y$ cents in coins, making the total $(100x + 2y)$ cents.

On arrival back home he had left $(100x + 2y)/3$ cents, so
  Fiona left him $[(100x + 2y)/3 - 50]$ cents.
Say this was y dollars and x cents, totaling $(x + 100y)$ ¢.
Then, $(100x + 2y - 150)/3 = x + 100y$,
  whence $97x - 298y = 150$,
  with general solution: $x = 298k + 106$, $y = 97k + 34$.
Then, $100x + 2y = 29994k + 10668$.
Two-thirds of that is $19996k + 7112$, which was less than
  10000.
So here we require $k = 0$, making $x = 106$, $2y = 68$.
Stan started with $106.68.

76. A MATTER OF AGES

Ages: Ted x years, Robin y, Pat z, all integral, $x > y$.
Thence, $x^2 - y^2 = z^3$; and $x/y = y/z$, whence $y^2 = xz$.
Substituting for y^2 we have $x^2 - xz = z^3$, so $x(x - z) = z^3$.

That equation is fully satisfied by: $x - z = mz$,
  and $x = z^2/m$, where m is any rational number.
Thence, $z = z^2/m - mz$, so $z = m(m + 1)$.
Substituting for z, we have $x = m(m + 1)^2$, whence $y^2 = m^2(m + 1)^3$, which entails $y = m\sqrt{(m + 1)^3}$.
Now, y is an integer, so here we see m must be an integer.
Then, $(m + 1)$ must be a square, so say $m + 1 = n^2$.
Thence, $m = n^2 - 1$, and substituting we have:
  $x = n^4(n^2 - 1)$, $y = n^3(n^2 - 1)$, $z = n^2(n^2 - 1)$.

Obviously, $n > 1$. Also, for possible human ages, $n < 3$, so
  $n = 2$, whence ages were: Ted 48 years, Robin 24 years,
  Pat 12 years.

77. DROPPING IN ON LEN

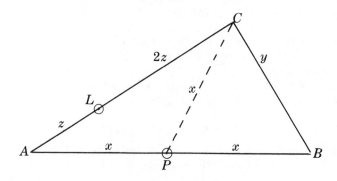

$PA = PB = PC$, so A, B, and C all lie on a circle with
center at P. AB is straight, so must be the diameter of
that circle, making the angle at C a right angle.

Then, $(2x)^2 = (3z)^2 + y^2$.
Also, $x + z = 23$, whence $5z^2 + 184z + y^2 = 2116$,
  hence $(5z + 92)^2 + 5y^2 = 4 \cdot 69^2$.
$69^2 = (8^2 + 5 \cdot 1^2)(8^2 + 5 \cdot 1^2) = (8^2 + 5 \cdot 1^2)(7^2 + 5 \cdot 2^2)$
  $= (7^2 + 5 \cdot 2^2)(7^2 + 5 \cdot 2^2)$
  $= 59^2 + 5 \cdot 16^2 = 46^2 + 5 \cdot 23^2 = 66^2 + 5 \cdot 9^2 = 29^2 + 5 \cdot 28^2$.

Thence, $5z + 92 = 118$ or 92 or 132 or 58
    making $z = $ — 0 8 —
    with $y = $ — 46 18 —
So it is 18 miles from Brent to Crowe as the crow flies.

78. CARDS ON THE TABLE

Say tabletop in square ¼-inches was $(x + 4)$ by x.
Each card had area 126 square ¼-inches.
He had an even number of surplus cards, so we may say:
  $(52 - 2y)$ cards occupied $252(26 - y)$ square ¼-inches.
But he had 180 square ¼-inches of wasted space.
So, $x(x + 4) = 252(26 - y) + 180$,
  whence $(x + 2)^2 = 6736 - 252y$.
Thence $(x + 2)^2 \equiv 6736 \pmod{252}$,
  so $(x + 2)^2 \equiv 4 \pmod 9 \equiv 2 \pmod 7$ and is even.
Thence, $(x + 2) \equiv \pm 11$ or $\pm 25 \pmod{63}$ and is even.

But $(x + 2)^2 < 6736$, so $(x + 2) < 83$.
Also $y < 14$, so $(x + 2)^2 > 3208$, hence $(x + 2) > 56$.
So we must have $(x + 2) = 74$, making $x = 72$.
Thence, $y = 5$.
The tabletop was 18 inches by 19 inches.

79. A BUS RIDE

Starting with x passengers, the numbers carried for each
  of the 5 successive stages were: x, $(2x + 15)/3$, $(4x + 48)/$
  9, $(2x + 60)/9$, $(x + 39)/9$.
Total number of different passengers was $(x + 12)$.
Total number of passenger-stage units was $(22x + 192)/9$,
  but that was an integer, so say $x = 9y + 6$.
Thence total different passengers was $(9y + 18)$, total

passenger-stage units was $(22y + 36)$, total fares in dollars $(9y + 18)$.

Say, z adult passenger-stage units, $(22y + 36 - z)$ child passenger-stage units.

Then, total fares would be $z/2 + (22y + 36 - z)/4$ dollars.

Thence, $(z + 22y + 36)/4 = 9y + 18$, so $z = 14y + 36$.

But one-fifth of all the different passengers were children, so $(9y + 18)$ is a multiple of 5,

making $y = (5w + 3)$, say.

Thence, $z = 70w + 78$.

At the start there were x passengers, and $x = 9y + 6$, so the bus started with $(45w + 33)$, "fewer than 60" passengers.

So $w = 0$, making $x = 33$, with $y = 3, z = 78$.

Then there were 45 passengers, one-fifth being children. So there were 36 adult passengers.

80. YOU'RE SURE IF IN DOUBT

One child must have been less than 4 years old.
Tabulate all factors of 96 in sets of three:

	24	16	12	16	12	8	8	6
	4	6	8	3	4	6	4	4
	1	1	1	2	2	2	3	4
Totals	29	23	21	21	18	16	15	14

Now, Ted obviously knew the number of the house. The fact that he was still in doubt shows that the ages must have totaled 21.

But, if the ages had been "16, 3, 2" there would have been only one child 4 years previously.

Hence, the ages must have been 12, 8, and 1 years.

81. CREEPY CRAWLIES

Say x children, y slugs.

Indicate individual children as: A got a slugs,
$\qquad\qquad\qquad\qquad\qquad\qquad$ B got b slugs,
$\qquad\qquad\qquad\qquad\qquad\qquad$ C got c slugs, etc.

Then A received $10a - 3(y - a) = 13a - 3y$,

$\qquad$ B received $(13b - 3y)$, and so on.

Total net amount received by the children:

$13(a + b + c + \ldots) - 3xy$, where $y = (a + b + c + \ldots)$

So, $13y - 3xy = 95x$, whence $(13 - 3x)(95 + 3y) = 13 \cdot 95$

Tabulate for factors: [NOTE: $(13 - 3x) < 8$]

$$
\begin{array}{rcc}
13 - 3x = & 5 & 1 \\
95 + 3y = & 247 & 1235 \\
x = & — & 4 \\
y = & — & 380
\end{array}
$$

So, 380 slugs were collected by 4 children.

A possible breakdown of the totals would be:

A got 92: received net \$9.20–\$8.64, i.e., \$0.56

B got 94: received net \$9.40–\$8.58, i.e., \$0.82

C got 96: received net \$9.60–\$8.52, i.e., \$1.08

D got 98: received net \$9.80–\$8.46, i.e., \$1.34.

82. FAMILY NUMBERS

Say Doug's special divisor was x, the remainder being y
  in each case.

Then say: $\quad\quad$ ax + y = 9638

$\quad\quad\quad\quad\quad$ bx + y = 8739

$\quad\quad\quad\quad\quad$ cx + y = 2591

Subtracting: $\quad$ x(a − b) = 899 = 29·31

$\quad\quad\quad\quad\quad$ x(b − c) = 6148 = 4·29·53

The common factor is 29, so x = 29.

Doug divided each number by 29, with remainder 10 in
  each case.

83. TOO MANY GIRLS

Say there were x girls, each scoring $y/2$ points, and 2 boys.

Then there were $(x + 1)(x + 2)/2$ games in all, and there
  were $(x + 1)(x + 2)/2$ points in all.

But the total number of points was $xy/2 + 9$.

So $(x + 1)(x + 2) = xy + 18$, whence $(2x - y)^2 + 12x = y^2 + 64$.

Say $(2x - y) = X$, making $(X + 3)^2 - (y - 3)^2 = 64$.

$$
\begin{array}{lrccc}
\text{Thence:} & [(X + 3) + (y - 3)]/2 = & 4 & 8 & 16 \\
\text{with} & [(X + 3) - (y - 3)]/2 = & 4 & 2 & 1 \\
\hline
\text{making} & (X + 3) \quad\quad\quad\quad = & 8 & 10 & 17 \\
\text{and} & (y - 3) = & 0 & 6 & 15 \\
\hline
\text{whence} & x = & 4 & 8 & 16 \\
\text{with} & y = & 3 & 9 & 18
\end{array}
$$

But "the girls all did better than either of us," and the
two boys totaled 9 points in all. Hence $y/2 > 9/2$, $y > 9$.

So we must have $x = 16$, with $y = 18$.
Hence there were 16 girls, each scoring 9 points, (i.e., each
girl played 2 games against boys, 15 against girls).

84. WHAT? NO ZOBBLIES?

Say $5x$ at 97¢ for 5 ....97x ¢,
$\quad$ $3y$ at 67¢ for 3 ....67y ¢,
$\quad$ $(100 - 5x - 3y)$ at 25¢ ....25$(100 - 5x - 3y)$ ¢.
Then $25(100 - 5x - 3y) + 97x + 67y = 2000$,
$\quad$ whence $7x + 2y = 125$, with general integral solutions:
$\quad$ $x = 2k + 1$, $y = 59 - 7k$.
That entails $(5x + 3y) = 182 - 11k < 100$, so here we must
$\quad$ have $k > 7$. But, re y, $k < 9$.
So $k = 8$, making $x = 17$, $y = 3$, $5x = 85$, $3y = 9$.

Hence, 6 zobblies were sold at 25¢ each.

85. THE CENSUS

Say $(3x)^2/3$ cats, i.e., $3x^2$.
Then, if a quarter were slain, $9x^2/4$ would remain.
So, $9x^2/4 = y^3$, say, so $(3x/2)^2 = y^3$.
Thence, $y = k^2$, say.
But y must be a multiple of 3, hence $k = 3t$, say.
Thence, $(3x/2) = 27t^3$, so $x = 18t^3$, $y = 9t^2$.

For minimal number of cats we must have $t = 1$, with $x = 18$.
Hence there were at least 972 cats.

86. A WHIZ KID

Say $7x$ questions, $(7x - y)$ answered correctly.
Then $7(7x - y) - y(y + 1)/2 = 168$, x and y being integers.
Thence $\quad$ $y(y + 15) = 98x - 336$,
$\quad$ whence $\quad$ $(2y + 15)^2 = 392x - 1119$, and $392 = 49 \cdot 8$,
$\quad$ so $\quad$ $(2y + 15)^2 \equiv 8(\bmod 49) \equiv 400(\bmod 49)$ and is odd.
Hence $\quad$ $(2y + 15) \equiv \pm 29(\bmod 98)$.
The boy answered more than three-quarters correctly, so
$\quad$ we require $7x > 4y$.

With $(2y + 15) = 29$, we have $y = 7$, $x = 5$, which is acceptable.

With $(2y + 15) = 69$, we have $y = 27$, $x = 15$, not acceptable.

With $(2y + 15) = 127$, and in all greater cases, the x/y ratio would be acceptable, but the numbers of questions would be quite unrealistic.

Hence we have $x = 5$, with $y = 7$.

There were 35 questions, and John answered 28 correctly.

87. TICKETS IN THE SWEEP

Say Susan had numbers $(x - 1)$, x, and $(x + 1)$, Jack had number y, Jill number z.

Then, $(x - 1)^2 + y^2 = (x + 1)^2$, whence $y^2 = 4x$.

So, $x = k^2$ and $y = 2k$, where k is an integer.

We also have $x^2 + z^2 = (x + 1)^2$, whence $z^2 = 2x + 1$.

Hence, $z^2 = 2k^2 + 1$, making $z^2 - 2k^2 = 1$.   (A)

We have $x < 1000$, so $k < 32$.

Within those limits equation (A) has only two non-zero integral solutions.

With $z = 3$, $k = 2$, we have $x = y = 4$, which is unacceptable because all ticket numbers were different.

So $z = 17$, $k = 12$, making $x = 144$, $y = 24$.

Susan had numbers 143, 144, 145; Jack 24, Jill 17.

88. PROGRESS

Say the odd house numbers ran from 1 to $(2m - 1)$, and the numbers of the houses purchased ran from $(2n + 1)$ to 43, all being odd.

$$\text{Sum } 1 \text{ to } (2n - 1) = n^2$$
$$\text{Sum } 45 \text{ to } (2m - 1) = m^2 - 484$$
$$\text{Sum } 1 \text{ to } (2m - 1) = m^2$$

So, $n^2 + m^2 - 484 = m^2/2$,
    whence $m^2 + 2n^2 = 968$.

Say $m = 2M$, $n = 2N$, making $M^2 + 2N^2 = 242$, with solution $M = 12$, $N = 7$, whence $m = 24$, $n = 14$.

So the odd numbers ran from 1 to 47 inclusive.

The houses that were bought ran from 29 to 43, all odd.

89. THREE TIMES

Say $N = 100x + y$, where x has n digits and $y < 100$.
Then, $10^n y + x = 300x + 3y$, whence $(10^n - 3)y = 299x$.
$299 = 23 \cdot 13$, so: $(10^n - 3) \equiv 0(\bmod\ 13)$ or $0(\bmod\ 23)$ or $0(\bmod\ 299)$.

Say $10^n \equiv 3(\bmod\ 13)$. We have $10^4 \equiv 3(\bmod\ 13)$, so for minimal values $n = 4$.
Thence, $299x = 9997y$, whence $x = 769k$, $y = 23k$, say.
But x must have 4 digits, and y must be odd. Hence $k = 3$, making $x = 2307$, $y = 69$. $N = 230769$.

Say $10^n \equiv 3(\bmod\ 23)$. All to $(\bmod\ 23)$ we have $10^2 \equiv 8$, $10^3 \equiv 11$, $10^4 \equiv -5$, $10^5 \equiv -4$, $10^6 \equiv 6$, etc.
Hence this case would entail N greater than 230769.

Say $10^n \equiv 3(\bmod\ 299)$. All to $(\bmod\ 299)$ we have $10^3 \equiv 103$, $10^4 \equiv 133$, $10^5 \equiv 134$, $10^6 \equiv 144$, etc.
Hence this case would entail N greater than 230769.

So Bill's number was 230769.

90. A TOUCHING TALE

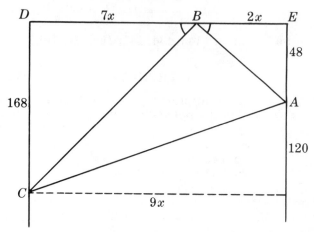

Referring to the diagram, for minimal $(AB + BC)$ we must have angles ABE and CBD equal, so $EB/BD = 48/168 = 2/7$.

So say $EB = 2x$, $BD = 7x$, making $AB =$
$2\sqrt{x^2 + 576}$, $BC = 7\sqrt{x^2 + 576}$, $AC = 3\sqrt{9x^2 + 1600}$,
whence $AB + BC = 9\sqrt{x^2 + 576} = 3\sqrt{9x^2 + 1600} + 48$.

So, $\sqrt{9x^2 + 5184} \quad - \quad \sqrt{9x^2 + 1600} \quad = \quad 16$,   (1)
But, $(9x^2 + 5184) \quad - \quad (9x^2 + 1600) = 3584$.   (2)
Divide (2) by (1):
     $\sqrt{9x^2 + 5184} \quad + \quad \sqrt{9x^2 + 1600} \quad = \quad 224$.   (3)
Adding (1) to (3): $2\sqrt{9x^2 + 5184} \qquad = \quad 240$.
So $\sqrt{9x^2 + 5184} = 120$, whence $x = 32$.
Hence the square field had sides 288 feet, area 82944
  square feet.

91. FUN FOR SOME

Ages: Jack y, Martha x. Then, $3y^2 - 2x^2 = 100x + y$,
  whence $(6y - 1)^2 - 6(2x + 50)^2 = -14999 = -283 \cdot 53$,
  so $(6y - 1)^2 - 6(2x + 50)^2 = (17^2 - 6 \cdot 1^2)(1^2 - 6 \cdot 3^2)$
  $= (17 \pm 18)^2 - 6(51 \pm 1)^2$
  $= 1^2 - 6 \cdot 50^2$ or $35^2 - 6 \cdot 52^2$.

Re $(1^2 - 6 \cdot 50^2)$: $6y - 1 = \pm(m \pm 300n)$
              $2x + 50 = 50m \pm n$
  where $m^2 - 6n^2 = 1$.
Tabulating: $m = 1 \quad 5 \qquad 5$ etc.
              $n = 0 \quad 2 \qquad 2$ etc.
              $y = - \quad - \quad 101$ etc.
              $x = - \quad - \quad 101$ etc.
But we require $x < 100$ (i.e., 2-digit integer).

Re $(35^2 - 6 \cdot 52^2)$: $6y - 1 = \pm(35m \pm 312n)$
              $2x + 50 = 52m \pm 35n$
  where $m^2 - 6n^2 = 1$.
Tabulating: $m = 1 \quad 5 \quad 5 \quad 49$ etc.
              $n = 0 \quad 2 \quad 2 \quad 20$ etc.
              $y = 6 \quad 75 \quad - \quad -$ etc.
              $x = 1 \quad 70 \quad - \quad -$ etc.
Obviously the ages were: Jack 75, Martha 70 years.

92. HE BROKE THE BANK

Say, $[x(x + y) - 288]$ quarters, x dimes, y nickels, $x(x + y)$
  pennies.
The only even prime number is 2.

If $x = 2$, there would be $(2y - 284)$ quarters. For that to
  be prime, we would require $y = 143$, composite.
If $y = 2$, there would be $[(x + 1)^2 - 289]$ quarters, i.e.,
  $(x + y - 17)(x + y + 17)$, composite.

Also, $x(x + y) - 288$ must be prime.
Since x and y are both odd primes, $[x(x + y) - 288]$ must
  be even. Hence, $x(x + y) - 288 = 2$, $x(x + y) = 290$.
Then, $290 = 2 \cdot 5 \cdot 29$, and $(x + y)$ is even.
Tabulating for factors:

	$x + y = 290$	58
with	$x = \ \ 1$	5
making	$y = 289$	53

But both x and y must be prime, so we have $x = 5, y = 53$.
There were 2 quarters, 5 dimes, 53 nickels, 290 pennies,
  a total of $6.55.

93. DO IT YOURSELF

We have, say, $x^2 + y^2 = z^2$, and $w^2 + 23^2 = 2z^2$, where x, y,
  z are integers, and z^2 is "getting on for 1500."
Then, $w^2 - 2z^2 = -529$ with two distinct basic solutions:
$$w = 23, z = 23, \quad \text{AND} \quad w = 7, z = 17.$$
So all solutions will stem from two "families."

Re $(w; z) = (23; 23)$ we have: $w = \pm 23(m \pm 2n)$,
  $z = 23(m \pm n)$, where $m^2 - 2n^2 = 1$.
But, $z^2 < 1500$, hence $z < 39$, so $(m \pm n) < 2$. That restricts
  us to $w = 23, z = 23$, which is not acceptable because it
  would lead to $x^2 + y^2 = 529$ which can have no integral
  solution (i.e., 23 being of form $[4r - 1]$).

Re $(w; z) = (7; 17)$ we have: $w = \pm(7m \pm 34n)$,
  $z = (17m \pm 7n)$, where $m^2 - 2n^2 = 1$.
With $m = 1, n = 0$, we have $w = 7, z = 17$. But we require
  z^2 to be "getting on for 1500."
With the next larger pair of (m, n) values, $m = 3, n = 2$,
  we have $w = 47, z = 37$, and $37^2 = 1369$.

Then, since $1369 = 12^2 + 35^2$, Joe's new tables would have
  144 and 1225 tiles respectively, a total of 1369 tiles.

94. A BUG FOR THE BIRDS

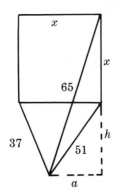 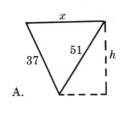 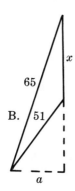

A.

B.

Area of triangle with sides x, y, z is:
$\sqrt{s(s-x)(s-y)(s-z)}$ where $x + y + z = 2s$.
Hence area of triangle A is $\sqrt{(88^2 - x^2)(x^2 - 196)}/4 = xh/2$,
and area of triangle B is $\sqrt{(116^2 - x^2)(x^2 - 196}/4 = xa/2$.
So $(88^2 - x^2)(x^2 - 196) = 4x^2h^2$.
and $(116^2 - x^2)(x^2 - 196) = 4x^2a^2$.
But $a^2 + h^2 = 51^2 = 2601$, hence $4x^2(a^2 + h^2) = 10404x^2$.
Thence, $(x^2 - 196)(88^2 - x^2 + 116^2 - x^2) = 10404x^2$,
whence $x^4 - 5594x^2 + 2077600 = 0$,
so $x^2 = 2797 \pm 2397$.

With $x^2 = 5194$, the bug would have to be right on the feeder tray which, incidentally, would be unduly large.
So we have $x^2 = 400$, making $x = 20$.
The feeder tray had 20-inch sides.

95. A LUCKY NUMBER

Say: $N = 10^5a + 10^4b + 10^3c + 10^2d + 10e + f$
and $kN = 10^5f + 10^4e + 10^3d + 10^2c + 10b + a$.
Then, $10^5(ak - f) + 10^4(bk - e) + 10^3(ck - d) + 10^2(dk - c) + 10(ek - b) + fk = a$, whence $fk = 10t + a$, where $t < 9$, with $(f - k) < ak \leq f$, and $ak < 10, f < 10$.
Obviously, if k is even, a will be even, also $k > 1$, so $a < 5$. Hence, $a = 4, 3, 2$, or 1.
All requirements are met only with: $a = 2, k = 4, fk = 32$, $f = 8$ OR $a = 1, k = 9, fk = 81, f = 9$.

Say, $a = 1, k = 9, f = 9$.
Then $10^4(9b - e) + 10^3(9c - d) + 10^2(9d - c) + 10(9e - b) + 80 = 0$,
  whence $8999b + 890c = 991e + 10d - 8$.
But maximum $(991e + 10d - 8) = 9001$, so $b = 0$.
Then, $890c = 991e + 10d - 8$, entailing $e = 8$.
Thence, $89c - d = 792$, so $c = 9, d = 9. N = 109989$.

Say, $a = 2, k = 4, f = 8$.
Then $1333b + 130c + 1 = 20d + 332e$.
But maximum $(20d + 332e) = 3168$, so $b < 3$. Also, $(1333b + 1)$ must be even, so b must be odd, hence $b = 1$.
Then, $10d + 166e = 65c + 667$. But maximum $(65c + 667) = 1352$, so $e < 8$. Also, we require $(10d + 166e) > 666$. So $e > 2$.
But $(166e - 667)$ must be divisible by 5, hence $e = 7$.
Thence, $13c - 2d = 99$, so $d = 9, c = 9. N = 219978$.
So $219978 \cdot 4 = 879912$.

96. A MATTER OF TIME

Say he went out at z hours, w minutes.
The hour hand was at $(60z + w)/12$ minutes, minute hand at w.
Say he returned at x hours, y minutes.
The hour hand was at $(60x + y)/12$ minutes, minute hand at y.

Then, $y = (60z + w)/12$, and $(60x + y)/12 = w + 2$.
Combining the two equations:
$$60z = 143w + 288 - 720x.$$
But y is an integer, so $w = 12k$, say, k being some integer.
Then $5z + 60x = 143k + 24$.
But k is an integer, and obviously $k < 5$,
  so $k = 2$, making $z + 12x = 62$.
Then, since $z \le 12$, we have $z = 2$, with $x = 5$.
Thence, $y = 12$, and $w = 24$.

He went out at 2:24 p.m., returning at 5:12 p.m.

97. THE POSTER

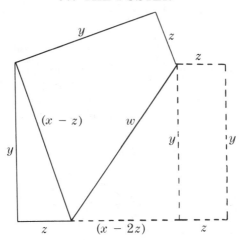

$(x - z)^2 = y^2 + z^2$, whence $z = (x^2 - y^2)/2x$.
Then, $x - 2z = y^2/x$,
so $w^2 = (x - 2z)^2 + y^2 = (y^4 + x^2y^2)/x^2$,
making $w = \dfrac{y\sqrt{(x^2 + y^2)}}{x}$.

Here we have $y = 120$, $w = 136$,
so $136x = 120\sqrt{x^2 + 14400}$, whence $x = 225$.
The poster was 225 cm long.

98. AT THE CASINO

This problem is a variation on the classic problem of the odds against two people in a certain group having the same birthday:

"Say there are n people in a room. What is the probability that at least two of them have the same birthday in the year (i.e., same date in the year, not necessarily the same year)?"

Ignoring February 29th, a possible leap year birthday, the exact probability is given by:

$$1 - \frac{\lfloor 365}{365^n \cdot \lfloor (365 - n)}$$

In our roulette variation on the theme we have 37 numbers corresponding to 365 days, and n spins corresponding to n people. Odds of "3 to 1 against" means probability $\frac{1}{4}$.

So, we have $1 - \dfrac{\lfloor 37}{37^n \cdot \lfloor (37 - n)} = \dfrac{1}{4}$ approximately.

With $n = 4$ we have probability 0.15424 approximately,
with $n = 5$, probability is approximately 0.24566,
with $n = 6$, probability is approximately 0.34761.
Hence there had been 5 spins of the wheel.

99. NO DIRECT ROAD

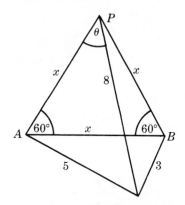

$\cos \theta = (x^2 + 64 - 25)/16x = (x^2 + 39)/16x$.
$\sin^2\theta = 1 - (x^2 + 39)^2/256x^2 = -(x^4 - 178x^2 + 1521)/256x^2$.
$\sin \theta = \dfrac{\sqrt{178x^2 - x^4 - 1521}}{16x}$.

Also, $\cos (60° - \theta) = (x^2 + 64 - 9)/16x = (x^2 + 55)/16x$.
But, $\cos (60° - \theta) = \cos 60°\cos\theta + \sin 60°\sin\theta$,
   so $(x^2 + 55)/16x = (x^2 + 39)/32x + \sqrt{3(178x^2 - x^4 - 1521)}/32x$,
whence $x^4 - 98x^2 + 2401 = 0$, and $x = 7$.
So the villages were 7 miles apart.

100. A NEST EGG

Say the mother's age was m years when Mary was 1 year old.
Then, when Mary's age was n years, Geoffrey deposited $n(m + n - 1)$ dollars.

Tabulate for the first few years:

Year	Deposit	Accumulated Deposits
1	m	$m + 0$
2	$2m + 2$	$3m + 2$
3	$3m + 6$	$6m + 8$
4	$4m + 12$	$10m + 20$

It can be seen that when Mary's age was n years, the total deposits would amount to $n(n + 1)(3m + 2n - 2)/6$.
So, $n(n + 1)(3m + 2n - 2) = 888 \cdot 6 = 2^4 \cdot 3^2 \cdot 37$.

n and $(n + 1)$ are consecutive integers, so each must be a factor of $2^4 \cdot 3^2 \cdot 37$. Also we may assume $m > 12$, so $n < 10$.

Then there are only 3 possible values for n giving:

$$n(n + 1) = 2 \cdot 3 \qquad 3 \cdot 4 \qquad 8 \cdot 9$$
$$\text{making} \quad m \;\; = 886/3 \quad 440/3 \quad 20$$

Hence her mother was 19 years old when Mary was born.

ALPHAMETICS

1.

```
      L I N G
  K W O N G
      L E E
  L I K E E
  ─────────
  L I C H E E
```

2. Little crosses indicate digits you will have to identify. There is no "remainder."

```
x x x ) x x x x x x ( x 8 x
        x x x x
        ─────────
          x x x x
          x 8 x
          ─────────
            x x x x
            x x x x
            ─────────
              ─ ─ ─ ─
```

3.

```
  N I N E
  L E S S
  T W O
  ─────────
  S E V E N
```

Two is the only even prime number, and here our TWO is truly prime!

4.

```
  A N D
  S O
  T O
  B E D
  S A Y D
  ─────────
  P E P Y S
```

Long, long ago in "ye olde England"! But don't forget our PEPYS was odd.

5.

```
    K A T E ' S
    K I T T E N
    H A T E S
    T H E S E
    _____

    S T E A K S
```

Well, well!
The **STEAKS**
must be odd.

6.

```
    K N O C K
    K N O C K
    I T ' S
    T H E
    _____

    P O S T I E
```

7.

```
        P E T E R
        P O P P L E
        P E D D L E S
        C O P P E R
        _____

        K E T T L E S
```

8. Little crosses
indicate digits
you will have to
identify. There is
no "remainder."

```
x x x ) x x x x x x x x x ( x x 7 x x
        x x x
        _____

        x x x
        x x x
        _____

          x x x x
          x x x x
          _____

          - - - -
```

9.

They're beautiful
beasts with their
long tapered horns,
and in fact this
is a prime ORYX!

```
    O R Y X
    O R Y X
    R U N
    O N
    _____

    K A R O O
```

10.

That's where he lived,
of course. But Holmes
never solved problems
like this!

```
    R E S T
    B R E A K
    A T
    B A K E R
    _____

    S T R E E T
```

11.

```
    P A S H A ' S
    H U B B L E
    B U B B L E
    _____

    B U B B L E S
```

12.

```
    P R E T T Y
    P O L L Y
    P A R R O T
    _____

    R E P E A T S
```

13.
```
        W H Y        Hardly a
          O H        national
        ———          league
        W H Y        pitcher!
      L O B
      ———
      L A D Y
```

14.
```
If they rattle        S H A K E
it's ripe! So         S H A K E
our PIPPIN will         P I P S
not be odd.               I N
                    ———————————
                    P I P P I N
```

15.
```
We have only    x x x ) x x x x x x ( 7 x x
the one 7 in              x x x
this, and it's           ———
the 7 you see.           x x x x
No "remainder."          x x x x
                         ———————
                         – – – –
```

16.
```
        L I L Y        Sleek and sheer,
        L I K E S      of course, but
        S I L K Y      the NYLONS will
        S I L K Y      not be odd!
      ———————————
      N Y L O N S
```

17.
```
      P E T E R
      P A P E'S
            A
      P A P E R
      L I T T E R
      ———————————
      P I C K E R
```

18.
```
        S U S I E
          S E E S
              A
        B L U E
        B L U E
      ———————————
      B E E T L E
```

19. Here we square a
4-digit number.
The little crosses
indicate digits to
be identified.

```
      x x x x
      x x x x
    ───────────
    x x x x x
    x x x x x
    3 x x x
    x x x x
    ───────────
    x x x x x x 3 x
```

20.
```
    D I V E R
    D I V E S
      D E E P
        I N
    ───────────
    R I V E R
```
It could be dangerous,
what with weeds and
other snags. But that
DIVER is truly prime!

21. They're morons,
of course! But
it should be a
prime STREAK.

```
        S E E
      K O O K Y
      K O O K S
    ───────────
    S T R E A K
```

22.
```
    P E T E R
    P I P E R
    L I K E D
      R E D
      R E D
    ───────────
    P E P P E R
```

23.
```
    A D A M
    S A Y S
      Y E S
      I ' M
    A D A M
    ───────────
    M A D A M
```

24.
```
        x x x x
        x x 7 x
    ───────────
      x x x x x
      x x x x
    x x x x x
    ───────────
    x x x x x x x x
```
We have only the
one 7 in this, and
it's the 7 you see.

25. A tougher
variation
on the old classic
SEND MORE
MONEY
theme!

```
    M O N E Y
        P O P
      S O M E
    M O N E Y
    ───────────
    P L E A S E
```

26.
```
      A L L
        A
    R U D D Y
    R U D D Y
    ─────────
  M U D D L E
```
There's no real
muddle here, but
you should find
this **MUDDLE** odd!

27.
```
    W H E N
      I N
    R O M E
      B E
        A
    ─────────
  R O M A N
```

28.
```
      B O N G O
      B O N G O
      B O N G O
          O N
        T H E
      ─────────
    C O N G O
```

29.
```
    J E L L Y
    J E L L Y
      A L L
    W I L D
  W I B B L E
  ─────────────
  W O B B L E
```
That **JELLY** is
quite special!
In fact, it is
truly prime.

30. A "toughie."
     No "remainder."
```
  T H E ) F I S T S ( M A Y
          F L Y
          ─────
            x x x
            x x x
            ───────
          x x x x
          x x x x
          ───────────
          ─ ─ ─ ─
```

31.
```
    H O L M E S
    S O L V E D
      M O O D
    ───────────
  M U R D E R S
```
There were many
of that type, but
the **MURDERS** must
be truly odd!

32.
```
      M E I N
      P A P A
      L I L L I
      P A L M E R
      ───────────
    T R I L L E D
```

33.
```
    E S K I M O
        M I S S
      M I S S E S
          I C E
      ───────────
    I C I C L E S
```

34.
```
  F E M A L E S
         A T
       L A S T
   D E F E A T
   _____
   E V E R E S T
```

35.
```
   C R A B B Y
   C R A B B Y
   T A B B Y
       M A Y
   _____
   S C R A T C H
```

36.
```
   M E N
   A N D
   _____
   x x x
   x x x
   x x x
   _____
   W O M E N
```

37.
```
   S U S I E ' S
   S I S T E R
   S I S S I E
       S K I S
         I N
   S U S I E ' S
   _____
   B I K I N I S
```
With all that snow
BIKINIS must be odd!
That would make it
easier to solve, but
you really do not
need the information.

38.
```
   C H E F
   F R I E D
   O R D E R
   F O R
   _____
   F A T H E R
```

39.
```
   O L D
   S A L T
   T O L D
   T A L L
   _____
   T A L E S
```

40.
```
   B E A D Y
   E Y E D
   B L U E
   B U D G I E
   _____
   G U G G L E S
```

SOLUTIONS TO ALPHAMETICS

1.
```
    L I N G
K W O N G
    L E E
L I K E E
─────────
L I C H E E
```
In this and in many alphametics it is convenient to use the symbol → meaning "ends with." For example, 85 → 5. Also, if the letter O appears in the layout, the numeral 0 should be spelled out as "zero."

Here we have L = 1, and I = zero. Then in the LWI column, L + I = 1, so there is no carry from that column. Hence K = 9.

We have 2G + E → zero, hence E must be even. But, from the NNEE column, with E even we need an even carry from GGEE, so 2G + E = 20.

Now tabulate for possible E values, with corresponding values for G and other letters. Duplications or otherwise unacceptable values should be struck out or omitted.

E =	4		6	8
G =	8		7	6

2N + E → 8, so	N =	2	7	-	5
giving carry		1	2		2

I + L + K + carry	=	11	12	12

	O =	5	6	3	2
with	H =	6	7	5	4
giving carry		1	1	1	1

L + I + carry	=	2	2	2	2

$$W = \quad - \quad 3 \quad - \quad -$$
$$\text{with } C = \quad 5$$

Hence we have uniquely: 1028 + 93628 + 144 + 10944 = 105744.

2. x x x) x x x x x x (x 8 x   Re the 2nd product,
        x x x x   the divisor < 125.
       ————   Obviously, the
        x x x x   quotient is 989,
         x 8 x   so the divisor is
       ————   greater than 999/9,
        x x x x   i.e., > 111.
        x x x x
       ————
       – – – –

Considering the result of subtracting the 2nd product, we see it must start with 88 or 98.

If the 2nd product starts with 88, as a multiple of 8 it must be 888, impossible because the divisor > 111.

So the 2nd product starts with 98, and must be 984.

Hence the divisor is 123, and we have the complete calculation as: 121647 ÷ 123 = 989.

3. NINE LESS TWO SEVEN = 6862 4211 953 12026, with 9 and 8 interchangeable.

4. AND SO TO BED SAYD PEPYS = 237 94 64 507 9287 10189, with 3 and 6 interchangeable.

5. KATE'S KITTEN HATES THESE STEAKS = 25193 201198 75193 17939 319523.

6. KNOCK KNOCK IT'S THE POSTIE = 86728 86728 594 903 174953.

7. PETER POPPLE PEDDLES COPPER KETTLES = 10705 161190 1044903 861105 2077903.

8. 10007916 ÷ 124 = 80709.

9. ORYX ORYX RUN ON KAROO = 4987 4987 925 45 10944.

10. REST BREAK AT BAKER STREET = 5713 65742 43 64275 135773.

11. PASHA'S HUBBLE BUBBLE BUBBLES = 568968
    971120 171120 1711208.

12. PRETTY POLLY PARROT REPEATS = 715663
    79003 781196 1575862.

13. 314 × 21 = 6594.

14. SHAKE SHAKE PIPS IN PIPPIN = 64892 64892
    1316 30 131130.

15. 100536 ÷ 142 = 708.

16. LILY LIKES SILKY SILKY NYLONS = 5350
    53482 23540 23540 105912.

17. PETER PAPE'S A PAPER LITTER PICKER =
    36164 35367 5 35364 291164 398064.

18. SUSIE SEES A BLUE BLUE BEETLE = 89840
    8008 2 1390 1390 100630.

19. 3194 × 3194 = 10201636.

20. DIVER DIVES DEEP IN RIVER = 45179 45170
    4772 58 95179, with 0, 2, 8 interchangeable.

21. SEE KOOKY KOOKS STREAK = 144 76672 76671
    153487.

22. PETER PIPER LIKED RED RED PEPPER =
    12628 13128 93724 824 824 121128; 6, 7 interchangeable.

23. ADAM SAYS YES I'M ADAM MADAM = 5051 4534
    324 91 5051 15051, with 2 and 9 interchangeable.

24. 1238 × 8079 = 10001802.

25. MONEY POP SOME MONEY PLEASE = 96314 262
    8691 96314 201581.

26. ALL A RUDDY RUDDY MUDDLE = 433 4 62550
    62550 125537.

27. WHEN IN ROME BE A ROMAN = 9457 87 1065 25
    3 10637, with 2 and 8 interchangeable.

28. BONGO BONGO BONGO ON THE CONGO = 29719
    29719 29719 97 465 89719.

29. JELLY JELLY ALL WILD WIBBLE WOBBLE =
    39227 39227 522 1024 106629 186629.

30. 97848 ÷ 453 = 216.

31. HOLMES SOLVED MOOD MURDERS = 634129
    934820 1330 1570279.

32. MEIN PAPA LILLI PALMER TRILLED = 6835
    9494 73773 947680 1037782.

33. ESKIMO MISS MISSES ICE ICICLES = 789165
    6188 618878 147 1414378.

34. FEMALES AT LAST DEFEAT EVEREST =
    3497148 76 1786 543476 4042486.

35. CRABBY CRABBY TABBY MAY SCRATCH =
    964552 964552 34552 742 1964398.

36. 125 × 753 = 94125.

37. SUSIE'S SISTER SISSIE SKIS IN SUSIE'S
    BIKINIS = 919879 989470 989987 9289 85 919879
    3828589.

38. CHEF FRIED ORDER FOR FATHER = 7851 16453
    96356 196 120856.

39. OLD SALT TOLD TALL TALES = 394 8091 1394
    1099 10978.

40. BEADY EYED BLUE BUDGIE GUGGLES = 93256
    3635 9803 905143 1011837.

APPENDICES

APPENDIX I: DIOPHANTINE EQUATIONS

Diophantos, who lived during the third century A.D., was probably the first mathematician to make an extensive study of the types of equations that we now associate with his name. The salient feature of what are known as "diophantine equations" is that they involve two or more unknowns that in almost all cases represent integers.

The simplest such equation is known as the "Pell Equation":

$$X^2 - NY^2 = 1$$

where N is a non-square integer. There will be an infinite number of (X, Y) pairs of integral values satisfying this equation.

We have initially $X = 1$, $Y = 0$. Having determined the next greater pair of (X, Y) values, all further integral solutions are given by:

$$X_{n+2} = 2aX_{n+1} - X_n$$
$$Y_{n+2} = 2aY_{n+1} - Y_n$$

where a is the value of X in that "next greater" solution.

For example, the first two pairs of values for the equation $X^2 - 3Y^2 = 1$ are $(X, Y) = (1, 0)$ and $(2, 1)$, making $a = 2$. Then we can write down all successively greater pairs of values at sight:

$$X = 1 \quad 2 \quad 7 \quad 26 \quad 97 \quad \text{etc.}$$
$$Y = 0 \quad 1 \quad 4 \quad 15 \quad 56 \quad \text{etc.}$$

Then there is the more general form $X^2 - NY^2 = e$, where e is some positive or negative integer other than $+1$. This may include, as a particular case, $X^2 - NY^2 = -1$. For any particular value of N there will be integral solutions only for certain values of e, and vice versa. The theoretical problem of determining such *compatible* values for N and e is complex. But in practice the necessary confirmation as to whether or not integral solutions exist for any given N and e can be found by testing over a limited range of values for Y.

Let us assume that we have ascertained that there is an integral solution for $X^2 - NY^2 = e$, for particular values of N and e. And let us assume that this be the integral solution that involves minimal values $X = x$, $Y = y$. Also, let $X = m$, $Y = n$, be *any* integral solution of the Pell equation $X^2 - NY^2 = +1$, the N having the same value as in the original equation.

Then, $X^2 - NY^2 = e = x^2 - Ny^2$, and $m^2 - Nn^2 = 1$,

so $\quad X^2 - NY^2 = (x^2 - Ny^2)(m^2 - Nn^2)$
$$= x^2m^2 + N^2y^2n^2 - Nx^2n^2 - Ny^2m^2$$
$$= x^2m^2 \pm 2Nxymn + N^2y^2n^2 - Nx^2n^2$$
$$\mp 2Nxymn - Ny^2m^2$$
$$= (xm \pm Nyn)^2 - N(xn \pm ym)^2$$

Equating coefficients in the original $X^2 - NY^2 = e$, we have $X = xm \pm Nyn$, $Y = xn \pm ym$, the signs "+" or "−" being the same in each. Thence, substituting for m and n any pair of values that satisfied the equation $m^2 - Nn^2 = 1$, we obtain solutions for $X^2 - NY^2 = e$.

An example will make the procedure clear. Say $X^2 - 3Y^2 = -11$, the minimal integral solution of which is $X = 1$, $Y = 2$. Then other solutions are given by:
$$X = m \pm 6n, Y = n \pm 2m$$
But $(-X)^2 = (+X)^2$, and $(-Y)^2 = (+Y)^2$, so we may write this general solution more neatly as:
$$X = \pm(m \pm 6n), Y = \pm(2m \pm n)$$
where the internal signs agree, and m and n satisfy $m^2 - 3n^2 = 1$.

We can tabulate successive values of m and n, as already explained, writing down corresponding values of X and Y:

$m =$	1	2	2	7	7	26	26	etc.
$n =$	0	1	1	4	4	15	15	etc.
$X =$	1	4	8	17	31	64	116	etc.
$Y =$	2	3	5	10	18	37	67	etc.

This has been a very brief outline of the theoretical approach to the simplest types of diophantine equations. It may help the reader to understand what is involved in some of the detailed solutions to problems in this collection.

APPENDIX II: THAT REMAINDER BUSINESS

The mathematician calls it Congruence Theory, which may suggest something rather complicated. But here we look into some elementary aspects of this important branch of Number Theory in terms of the familiar remainder that may result from the process of simple division.

Congruence Theory, propounded and developed by the great Carl Gauss when he was still in his teens, is entailed in many popular-type mathematical teasers. To understand and apply its principles in the solving of such problems does not involve delving deeply into abstruse theoretical considerations. In this brief survey the emphasis will be on practical applications rather than on theory. We shall be dealing only with integers, i.e., whole numbers.

It is essential, of course, to use and understand the special notation. Dividing 23 by 7, say, we have remainder 2. This would be shown as:

$$23 \equiv 2(\bmod 7)$$

which is read in words as "23 is congruent to 2, to modulus 7." In other words, "23 leaves a remainder of 2 when divided by 7." Stretching our concept of remainder, obviously an infinite number of integers must be congruent to 2, to modulus 7. For example:

$$30 \equiv 2(\bmod 7) \qquad 2 \equiv 2(\bmod 7) \qquad -5 \equiv 2(\bmod 7)$$

In fact, all such integers are solutions of the equation $x = 7k + 2$, where k is any integer (positive, negative or zero). A few more examples will familiarize the reader with these ideas.

Now we have seen that, to modulus 7, the integers 23 and 2 are equivalent. If we multiply one side of our original congruence equation by 2 and the other side by 23, the new congruence must then be valid:

$$46 \equiv 46(\bmod 7) \qquad 529 \equiv 4(\bmod 7)$$

The first of these needs no comment, but notice the second for future reference.

Clearly, $12 \equiv -2(\bmod 7)$, and for example:

$$19 \equiv -2(\bmod 7) \qquad -2 \equiv -2(\bmod 7)$$

Since 19 and -2 are equivalent, to modulus 7, we may multiply one side of the first by 19, and its other side by -2, to obtain a new congruence equation:

$$361 \equiv 4(\bmod 7)$$

Note here that $361 = 19^2$, and earlier we had $529 = 23^2$.

Now, say we have the equation $x^2 - 4 = 7y$, where x and y are integers. This may be written as $x^2 \equiv 4 \pmod 7$, which is satisfied by the general integral solution $x = 7k \pm 2$, i.e., $x \equiv \pm 2 \pmod 7$. If only positive values are required we have an infinite sequence of such values: 2, 5, 9, 12, 16, 19, 23, etc.

In solving some problem we might derive the rather more complex equation $x^2 - 6x + 6 = 11y$, say. This becomes $(x - 3)^2 = 11y + 3$, so $(x - 3)^2 \equiv 3 \pmod{11}$. But, 25 $\equiv 3 \pmod{11}$, hence we have $(x - 3)^2 \equiv 25 \pmod{11}$, so $(x - 3) \equiv \pm 5 \pmod{11}$. Thence $x \equiv 8$ or $9 \pmod{11}$, making the general solution $x = 11k - 3$, or $x = 11k - 2$. Hence particular solutions are 8, 9, 19, 20, etc., with corresponding values for y.

At this point it is suggested that the reader write down a few typical equations of similar type, and derive the general integral solutions. It will probably be found that some have no integral solutions. Full discussion of such cases must be outside the scope of this survey. However, say we have an equation $X^2 \equiv a \pmod m$, equivalent to $X = mk + a$. Then, if there is an integral value of k that will make the right-hand side a perfect square, the smallest such value must lie within the range of integral values $k = 0$ to $k = m/2$. So, to find the required perfect square (if it does exist), it is only necessary to test for values of k within that range.

So far we have considered only examples with prime moduli. Now we take a case where the modulus is a power of 2. Say $X^2 \equiv 1 \pmod 8$. Then we need test only for $k < 5$ in $X^2 = 8k + 1$. We find $X \equiv \pm 1 \pmod 8$ or $X \equiv \pm 3 \pmod 8$. The first few positive values of X are therefore 1, 3, 5, etc., and we see that those two different solutions do in fact comprise all the odd numbers. Hence they can be combined as a single solution, $X \equiv \pm 1 \pmod 4$. Indeed the general solution of $X^2 \equiv 1 \pmod{2^n}$ for moduli that are powers of 2 is $X \equiv \pm 1 \pmod{2^{n-1}}$: an important point to remember.

Cases of more complex composite moduli must also be considered. In such cases the modulus must be broken down into its distinct prime factors (or powers thereof). Say, for example, that $X^2 \equiv 1 \pmod{135}$. This implies $X^2 \equiv 1 \pmod 5$ and $X^2 \equiv 1 \pmod{27}$, so we must find solutions in X that will satisfy both congruence equations.

In general, to deal with a composite modulus we first set up the requisite number of subsidiary congruence equations, depending on the number of prime factor elements in the modulus. Each of those subsidiary equations must be solved, using the methods that have been outlined, and finally those separate solutions will have to be coordinated to give the general solution that will cover all of them.

For example, say $X^2 \equiv 11 \pmod{35}$, the congruence equation that results from $X^2 - 11 = 35Y$. Here the modulus is $5 \cdot 7$, so $X^2 \equiv 11 \equiv 1 \pmod 5$, and $X^2 \equiv 11 \equiv 4 \pmod 7$, the distinct solutions being $X \equiv \pm 1 \pmod 5$ and $X \equiv \pm 2 \pmod 7$.

The simplest method for co-ordinating those two distinct solutions follows. It will be given in detail because its application is involved so often in solving problems that entail congruence equations.

Say $X = 5u + a = 7v + b$, where u and v are integers, with $a = \pm 1$ and $b = \pm 2$ (the $+$ and $-$ signs being independent). Dividing through by 5, it is seen that $(2v - a + b)/5$ must be an integer. Thence, $(v - 3a + 3b)/5$ must be an integer, say t. So $v = 5t + 3a - 3b$. But, $X = 7v + b$, so $X = 35t + 21a - 20b$, which implies $X \equiv [21a - 20b] \pmod{35}$.

Now we assign their values to a and b, getting $X \equiv [\pm 21 \pm 40] \pmod{35}$, the $+$ and $-$ signs being mutually independent. Thence $X \equiv \pm 9$ or $\pm 16 \pmod{35}$.

So the required general solution of $X^2 - 11 = 35Y$ is $X = 35k \pm 9$ or $X = 35k \pm 16$. The first few positive values for X being: 9, 16, 19, 26, 44, etc. If the basic equation was derived in the solving of a popular-type "teaser," there would be some special stipulation that would pinpoint one or more particular values.

Where the modulus has three or more different prime factor elements, precisely the same method is used. Having coordinated two of the subsidiary congruence solutions, the resulting solution is coordinated with the third, and so on. Try solving $X^2 - 4 = 105Y$, as a simple example.

A CATALOG OF SELECTED
DOVER BOOKS
IN ALL FIELDS OF INTEREST

A CATALOG OF SELECTED DOVER
BOOKS IN ALL FIELDS OF INTEREST

CONCERNING THE SPIRITUAL IN ART, Wassily Kandinsky. Pioneering work by father of abstract art. Thoughts on color theory, nature of art. Analysis of earlier masters. 12 illustrations. 80pp. of text. 5⅜ × 8½.   23411-8 Pa. $3.95

ANIMALS: 1,419 Copyright-Free Illustrations of Mammals, Birds, Fish, Insects, etc., Jim Harter (ed.). Clear wood engravings present, in extremely lifelike poses, over 1,000 species of animals. One of the most extensive pictorial sourcebooks of its kind. Captions. Index. 284pp. 9 × 12.   23766-4 Pa. $12.95

CELTIC ART: The Methods of Construction, George Bain. Simple geometric techniques for making Celtic interlacements, spirals, Kells-type initials, animals, humans, etc. Over 500 illustrations. 160pp. 9 × 12. (USO)   22923-8 Pa. $9.95

AN ATLAS OF ANATOMY FOR ARTISTS, Fritz Schider. Most thorough reference work on art anatomy in the world. Hundreds of illustrations, including selections from works by Vesalius, Leonardo, Goya, Ingres, Michelangelo, others. 593 illustrations. 192pp. 7⅞ × 10¼.   20241-0 Pa. $9.95

CELTIC HAND STROKE-BY-STROKE (Irish Half-Uncial from "The Book of Kells"): An Arthur Baker Calligraphy Manual, Arthur Baker. Complete guide to creating each letter of the alphabet in distinctive Celtic manner. Covers hand position, strokes, pens, inks, paper, more. Illustrated. 48pp. 8¼ × 11.

24336-2 Pa. $3.95

EASY ORIGAMI, John Montroll. Charming collection of 32 projects (hat, cup, pelican, piano, swan, many more) specially designed for the novice origami hobbyist. Clearly illustrated easy-to-follow instructions insure that even beginning papercrafters will achieve successful results. 48pp. 8¼ × 11.   27298-2 Pa. $2.95

THE COMPLETE BOOK OF BIRDHOUSE CONSTRUCTION FOR WOOD-WORKERS, Scott D. Campbell. Detailed instructions, illustrations, tables. Also data on bird habitat and instinct patterns. Bibliography. 3 tables. 63 illustrations in 15 figures. 48pp. 5¼ × 8½.   24407-5 Pa. $1.95

BLOOMINGDALE'S ILLUSTRATED 1886 CATALOG: Fashions, Dry Goods and Housewares, Bloomingdale Brothers. Famed merchants' extremely rare catalog depicting about 1,700 products: clothing, housewares, firearms, dry goods, jewelry, more. Invaluable for dating, identifying vintage items. Also, copyright-free graphics for artists, designers. Co-published with Henry Ford Museum & Greenfield Village. 160pp. 8¼ × 11.   25780-0 Pa. $9.95

HISTORIC COSTUME IN PICTURES, Braun & Schneider. Over 1,450 costumed figures in clearly detailed engravings—from dawn of civilization to end of 19th century. Captions. Many folk costumes. 256pp. 8⅜ × 11¾.   23150-X Pa. $11.95

STICKLEY CRAFTSMAN FURNITURE CATALOGS, Gustav Stickley and L. & J. G. Stickley. Beautiful, functional furniture in two authentic catalogs from 1910. 594 illustrations, including 277 photos, show settles, rockers, armchairs, reclining chairs, bookcases, desks, tables. 183pp. 6½ × 9¼. 23838-5 Pa. **$9.95**

AMERICAN LOCOMOTIVES IN HISTORIC PHOTOGRAPHS: 1858 to 1949, Ron Ziel (ed.). A rare collection of 126 meticulously detailed official photographs, called "builder portraits," of American locomotives that majestically chronicle the rise of steam locomotive power in America. Introduction. Detailed captions. xi + 129pp. 9 × 12. 27393-8 Pa. $12.95

AMERICA'S LIGHTHOUSES: An Illustrated History, Francis Ross Holland, Jr. Delightfully written, profusely illustrated fact-filled survey of over 200 American lighthouses since 1716. History, anecdotes, technological advances, more. 240pp. 8 × 10¾. 25576-X Pa. $11.95

TOWARDS A NEW ARCHITECTURE, Le Corbusier. Pioneering manifesto by founder of "International School." Technical and aesthetic theories, views of industry, economics, relation of form to function, "mass-production split" and much more. Profusely illustrated. 320pp. 6⅛ × 9¼. (USO) 25023-7 Pa. $9.95

HOW THE OTHER HALF LIVES, Jacob Riis. Famous journalistic record, exposing poverty and degradation of New York slums around 1900, by major social reformer. 100 striking and influential photographs. 233pp. 10 × 7⅞.
22012-5 Pa $10.95

FRUIT KEY AND TWIG KEY TO TREES AND SHRUBS, William M. Harlow. One of the handiest and most widely used identification aids. Fruit key covers 120 deciduous and evergreen species; twig key 160 deciduous species. Easily used. Over 300 photographs. 126pp. 5⅜ × 8½. 20511-8 Pa. $3.95

COMMON BIRD SONGS, Dr. Donald J. Borror. Songs of 60 most common U.S. birds: robins, sparrows, cardinals, bluejays, finches, more—arranged in order of increasing complexity. Up to 9 variations of songs of each species.
Cassette and manual 99911-4 $8.95

ORCHIDS AS HOUSE PLANTS, Rebecca Tyson Northen. Grow cattleyas and many other kinds of orchids—in a window, in a case, or under artificial light. 63 illustrations. 148pp. 5⅜ × 8½. 23261-1 Pa. $4.95

MONSTER MAZES, Dave Phillips. Masterful mazes at four levels of difficulty. Avoid deadly perils and evil creatures to find magical treasures. Solutions for all 32 exciting illustrated puzzles. 48pp. 8¼ × 11. 26005-4 Pa. $2.95

MOZART'S DON GIOVANNI (DOVER OPERA LIBRETTO SERIES), Wolfgang Amadeus Mozart. Introduced and translated by Ellen H. Bleiler. Standard Italian libretto, with complete English translation. Convenient and thoroughly portable—an ideal companion for reading along with a recording or the performance itself. Introduction. List of characters. Plot summary. 121pp. 5¼ × 8½.
24944-1 Pa. $2.95

TECHNICAL MANUAL AND DICTIONARY OF CLASSICAL BALLET, Gail Grant. Defines, explains, comments on steps, movements, poses and concepts. 15-page pictorial section. Basic book for student, viewer. 127pp. 5⅜ × 8½.
21843-0 Pa. $4.95

BRASS INSTRUMENTS: Their History and Development, Anthony Baines. Authoritative, updated survey of the evolution of trumpets, trombones, bugles, cornets, French horns, tubas and other brass wind instruments. Over 140 illustrations and 48 music examples. Corrected and updated by author. New preface. Bibliography. 320pp. 5⅜ × 8½. 27574-4 Pa. $9.95

HOLLYWOOD GLAMOR PORTRAITS, John Kobal (ed.). 145 photos from 1926–49. Harlow, Gable, Bogart, Bacall; 94 stars in all. Full background on photographers, technical aspects. 160pp. 8⅜ × 11¼. 23352-9 Pa. $11.95

MAX AND MORITZ, Wilhelm Busch. Great humor classic in both German and English. Also 10 other works: "Cat and Mouse," "Plisch and Plumm," etc. 216pp. 5⅜ × 8½. 20181-3 Pa. $5.95

THE RAVEN AND OTHER FAVORITE POEMS, Edgar Allan Poe. Over 40 of the author's most memorable poems: "The Bells," "Ulalume," "Israfel," "To Helen," "The Conqueror Worm," "Eldorado," "Annabel Lee," many more. Alphabetic lists of titles and first lines. 64pp. 5³⁄₁₆ × 8¼. 26685-0 Pa. $1.00

SEVEN SCIENCE FICTION NOVELS, H. G. Wells. The standard collection of the great novels. Complete, unabridged. First Men in the Moon, Island of Dr. Moreau, War of the Worlds, Food of the Gods, Invisible Man, Time Machine, In the Days of the Comet. Total of 1,015pp. 5⅜ × 8½. (USO) 20264-X Clothbd. $29.95

AMULETS AND SUPERSTITIONS, E. A. Wallis Budge. Comprehensive discourse on origin, powers of amulets in many ancient cultures: Arab, Persian, Babylonian, Assyrian, Egyptian, Gnostic, Hebrew, Phoenician, Syriac, etc. Covers cross, swastika, crucifix, seals, rings, stones, etc. 584pp. 5⅜ × 8½. 23573-4 Pa. $12.95

RUSSIAN STORIES/PYCCKNE PACCKA3bl: A Dual-Language Book, edited by Gleb Struve. Twelve tales by such masters as Chekhov, Tolstoy, Dostoevsky, Pushkin, others. Excellent word-for-word English translations on facing pages, plus teaching and study aids, Russian/English vocabulary, biographical/critical introductions, more. 416pp. 5⅜ × 8½. 26244-8 Pa. $8.95

PHILADELPHIA THEN AND NOW: 60 Sites Photographed in the Past and Present, Kenneth Finkel and Susan Oyama. Rare photographs of City Hall, Logan Square, Independence Hall, Betsy Ross House, other landmarks juxtaposed with contemporary views. Captures changing face of historic city. Introduction. Captions. 128pp. 8¼ × 11. 25790-8 Pa. $9.95

AIA ARCHITECTURAL GUIDE TO NASSAU AND SUFFOLK COUNTIES, LONG ISLAND, The American Institute of Architects, Long Island Chapter, and the Society for the Preservation of Long Island Antiquities. Comprehensive, well-researched and generously illustrated volume brings to life over three centuries of Long Island's great architectural heritage. More than 240 photographs with authoritative, extensively detailed captions. 176pp. 8¼ × 11. 26946-9 Pa. $14.95

NORTH AMERICAN INDIAN LIFE: Customs and Traditions of 23 Tribes, Elsie Clews Parsons (ed.). 27 fictionalized essays by noted anthropologists examine religion, customs, government, additional facets of life among the Winnebago, Crow, Zuni, Eskimo, other tribes. 480pp. 6⅛ × 9¼. 27377-6 Pa. $10.95

FRANK LLOYD WRIGHT'S HOLLYHOCK HOUSE, Donald Hoffmann. Lavishly illustrated, carefully documented study of one of Wright's most controversial residential designs. Over 120 photographs, floor plans, elevations, etc. Detailed perceptive text by noted Wright scholar. Index. 128pp. 9¼ × 10¾.
27133-1 Pa. $11.95

THE MALE AND FEMALE FIGURE IN MOTION: 60 Classic Photographic Sequences, Eadweard Muybridge. 60 true-action photographs of men and women walking, running, climbing, bending, turning, etc., reproduced from rare 19th-century masterpiece. vi + 121pp. 9 × 12.
24745-7 Pa. $10.95

1001 QUESTIONS ANSWERED ABOUT THE SEASHORE, N. J. Berrill and Jacquelyn Berrill. Queries answered about dolphins, sea snails, sponges, starfish, fishes, shore birds, many others. Covers appearance, breeding, growth, feeding, much more. 305pp. 5¼ × 8¼.
23366-9 Pa. $7.95

GUIDE TO OWL WATCHING IN NORTH AMERICA, Donald S. Heintzelman. Superb guide offers complete data and descriptions of 19 species: barn owl, screech owl, snowy owl, many more. Expert coverage of owl-watching equipment, conservation, migrations and invasions, etc. Guide to observing sites. 84 illustrations. xiii + 193pp. 5⅜ × 8½.
27344-X Pa. $8.95

MEDICINAL AND OTHER USES OF NORTH AMERICAN PLANTS: A Historical Survey with Special Reference to the Eastern Indian Tribes, Charlotte Erichsen-Brown. Chronological historical citations document 500 years of usage of plants, trees, shrubs native to eastern Canada, northeastern U.S. Also complete identifying information. 343 illustrations. 544pp. 6½ × 9¼.
25951-X Pa. $12.95

STORYBOOK MAZES, Dave Phillips. 23 stories and mazes on two-page spreads: Wizard of Oz, Treasure Island, Robin Hood, etc. Solutions. 64pp. 8¼ × 11.
23628-5 Pa. $2.95

NEGRO FOLK MUSIC, U.S.A., Harold Courlander. Noted folklorist's scholarly yet readable analysis of rich and varied musical tradition. Includes authentic versions of over 40 folk songs. Valuable bibliography and discography. xi + 324pp. 5⅜ × 8½.
27350-4 Pa. $7.95

MOVIE-STAR PORTRAITS OF THE FORTIES, John Kobal (ed.). 163 glamor, studio photos of 106 stars of the 1940s: Rita Hayworth, Ava Gardner, Marlon Brando, Clark Gable, many more. 176pp. 8⅜ × 11¼.
23546-7 Pa. $11.95

BENCHLEY LOST AND FOUND, Robert Benchley. Finest humor from early 30s, about pet peeves, child psychologists, post office and others. Mostly unavailable elsewhere. 73 illustrations by Peter Arno and others. 183pp. 5⅜ × 8½.
22410-4 Pa. $5.95

YEKL and THE IMPORTED BRIDEGROOM AND OTHER STORIES OF YIDDISH NEW YORK, Abraham Cahan. Film Hester Street based on Yekl (1896). Novel, other stories among first about Jewish immigrants on N.Y.'s East Side. 240pp. 5⅜ × 8½.
22427-9 Pa. $6.95

SELECTED POEMS, Walt Whitman. Generous sampling from *Leaves of Grass.* Twenty-four poems include "I Hear America Singing," "Song of the Open Road," "I Sing the Body Electric," "When Lilacs Last in the Dooryard Bloom'd," "O Captain! My Captain!"—all reprinted from an authoritative edition. Lists of titles and first lines. 128pp. 5³⁄₁₆ × 8¼.
26878-0 Pa. $1.00

THE BEST TALES OF HOFFMANN, E. T. A. Hoffmann. 10 of Hoffmann's most important stories: "Nutcracker and the King of Mice," "The Golden Flowerpot," etc. 458pp. 5⅜ × 8½. 21793-0 Pa. $8.95

FROM FETISH TO GOD IN ANCIENT EGYPT, E. A. Wallis Budge. Rich detailed survey of Egyptian conception of "God" and gods, magic, cult of animals, Osiris, more. Also, superb English translations of hymns and legends. 240 illustrations. 545pp. 5⅜ × 8½. 25803-3 Pa. $11.95

FRENCH STORIES/CONTES FRANÇAIS: A Dual-Language Book, Wallace Fowlie. Ten stories by French masters, Voltaire to Camus: "Micromegas" by Voltaire; "The Atheist's Mass" by Balzac; "Minuet" by de Maupassant; "The Guest" by Camus, six more. Excellent English translations on facing pages. Also French-English vocabulary list, exercises, more. 352pp. 5⅜ × 8½. 26443-2 Pa. $8.95

CHICAGO AT THE TURN OF THE CENTURY IN PHOTOGRAPHS: 122 Historic Views from the Collections of the Chicago Historical Society, Larry A. Viskochil. Rare large-format prints offer detailed views of City Hall, State Street, the Loop, Hull House, Union Station, many other landmarks, circa 1904–1913. Introduction. Captions. Maps. 144pp. 9⅜ × 12¼. 24656-6 Pa. $12.95

OLD BROOKLYN IN EARLY PHOTOGRAPHS, 1865–1929, William Lee Younger. Luna Park, Gravesend race track, construction of Grand Army Plaza, moving of Hotel Brighton, etc. 157 previously unpublished photographs. 165pp. 8⅞ × 11¾. 23587-4 Pa. $13.95

THE MYTHS OF THE NORTH AMERICAN INDIANS, Lewis Spence. Rich anthology of the myths and legends of the Algonquins, Iroquois, Pawnees and Sioux, prefaced by an extensive historical and ethnological commentary. 36 illustrations. 480pp. 5⅜ × 8½. 25967-6 Pa. $8.95

AN ENCYCLOPEDIA OF BATTLES: Accounts of Over 1,560 Battles from 1479 B.C. to the Present, David Eggenberger. Essential details of every major battle in recorded history from the first battle of Megiddo in 1479 B.C. to Grenada in 1984. List of Battle Maps. New Appendix covering the years 1967–1984. Index. 99 illustrations. 544pp. 6½ × 9¼. 24913-1 Pa. $14.95

SAILING ALONE AROUND THE WORLD, Captain Joshua Slocum. First man to sail around the world, alone, in small boat. One of great feats of seamanship told in delightful manner. 67 illustrations. 294pp. 5⅜ × 8½. 20326-3 Pa. $5.95

ANARCHISM AND OTHER ESSAYS, Emma Goldman. Powerful, penetrating, prophetic essays on direct action, role of minorities, prison reform, puritan hypocrisy, violence, etc. 271pp. 5⅜ × 8½. 22484-8 Pa. $5.95

MYTHS OF THE HINDUS AND BUDDHISTS, Ananda K. Coomaraswamy and Sister Nivedita. Great stories of the epics; deeds of Krishna, Shiva, taken from puranas, Vedas, folk tales; etc. 32 illustrations. 400pp. 5⅜ × 8½. 21759-0 Pa. $9.95

BEYOND PSYCHOLOGY, Otto Rank. Fear of death, desire of immortality, nature of sexuality, social organization, creativity, according to Rankian system. 291pp. 5⅜ × 8½. 20485-5 Pa. $8.95

A THEOLOGICO-POLITICAL TREATISE, Benedict Spinoza. Also contains unfinished Political Treatise. Great classic on religious liberty, theory of government on common consent. R. Elwes translation. Total of 421pp. 5⅜ × 8½. 20249-6 Pa. $8.95

MY BONDAGE AND MY FREEDOM, Frederick Douglass. Born a slave, Douglass became outspoken force in antislavery movement. The best of Douglass' autobiographies. Graphic description of slave life. 464pp. 5⅜ × 8½.   22457-0 Pa. $8.95

FOLLOWING THE EQUATOR: A Journey Around the World, Mark Twain. Fascinating humorous account of 1897 voyage to Hawaii, Australia, India, New Zealand, etc. Ironic, bemused reports on peoples, customs, climate, flora and fauna, politics, much more. 197 illustrations. 720pp. 5⅜ × 8½.   26113-1 Pa. $15.95

THE PEOPLE CALLED SHAKERS, Edward D. Andrews. Definitive study of Shakers: origins, beliefs, practices, dances, social organization, furniture and crafts, etc. 33 illustrations. 351pp. 5⅜ × 8½.   21081-2 Pa. $8.95

THE MYTHS OF GREECE AND ROME, H. A. Guerber. A classic of mythology, generously illustrated, long prized for its simple, graphic, accurate retelling of the principal myths of Greece and Rome, and for its commentary on their origins and significance. With 64 illustrations by Michelangelo, Raphael, Titian, Rubens, Canova, Bernini and others. 480pp. 5⅜ × 8½.   27584-1 Pa. $9.95

PSYCHOLOGY OF MUSIC, Carl E. Seashore. Classic work discusses music as a medium from psychological viewpoint. Clear treatment of physical acoustics, auditory apparatus, sound perception, development of musical skills, nature of musical feeling, host of other topics. 88 figures. 408pp. 5⅜ × 8½. 21851-1 Pa. $9.95

THE PHILOSOPHY OF HISTORY, Georg W. Hegel. Great classic of Western thought develops concept that history is not chance but rational process, the evolution of freedom. 457pp. 5⅜ × 8½.   20112-0 Pa. $9.95

THE BOOK OF TEA, Kakuzo Okakura. Minor classic of the Orient: entertaining, charming explanation, interpretation of traditional Japanese culture in terms of tea ceremony. 94pp. 5⅜ × 8½.   20070-1 Pa. $3.95

LIFE IN ANCIENT EGYPT, Adolf Erman. Fullest, most thorough, detailed older account with much not in more recent books, domestic life, religion, magic, medicine, commerce, much more. Many illustrations reproduce tomb paintings, carvings, hieroglyphs, etc. 597pp. 5⅜ × 8½.   22632-8 Pa. $10.95

SUNDIALS, Their Theory and Construction, Albert Waugh. Far and away the best, most thorough coverage of ideas, mathematics concerned, types, construction, adjusting anywhere. Simple, nontechnical treatment allows even children to build several of these dials. Over 100 illustrations. 230pp. 5⅜ × 8½.   22947-5 Pa. $7.95

DYNAMICS OF FLUIDS IN POROUS MEDIA, Jacob Bear. For advanced students of ground water hydrology, soil mechanics and physics, drainage and irrigation engineering, and more. 335 illustrations. Exercises, with answers. 784pp. 6⅛ × 9¼.   65675-6 Pa. $19.95

SONGS OF EXPERIENCE: Facsimile Reproduction with 26 Plates in Full Color, William Blake. 26 full-color plates from a rare 1826 edition. Includes "The Tyger," "London," "Holy Thursday," and other poems. Printed text of poems. 48pp. 5¼ × 7.   24636-1 Pa. $4.95

OLD-TIME VIGNETTES IN FULL COLOR, Carol Belanger Grafton (ed.). Over 390 charming, often sentimental illustrations, selected from archives of Victorian graphics—pretty women posing, children playing, food, flowers, kittens and puppies, smiling cherubs, birds and butterflies, much more. All copyright-free. 48pp. 9¼ × 12¼.   27269-9 Pa. $5.95

PERSPECTIVE FOR ARTISTS, Rex Vicat Cole. Depth, perspective of sky and sea, shadows, much more, not usually covered. 391 diagrams, 81 reproductions of drawings and paintings. 279pp. 5⅜ × 8½. 22487-2 Pa. $6.95

DRAWING THE LIVING FIGURE, Joseph Sheppard. Innovative approach to artistic anatomy focuses on specifics of surface anatomy, rather than muscles and bones. Over 170 drawings of live models in front, back and side views, and in widely varying poses. Accompanying diagrams. 177 illustrations. Introduction. Index. 144pp. 8⅜ × 11¼. 26723-7 Pa. $8.95

GOTHIC AND OLD ENGLISH ALPHABETS: 100 Complete Fonts, Dan X. Solo. Add power, elegance to posters, signs, other graphics with 100 stunning copyright-free alphabets: Blackstone, Dolbey, Germania, 97 more—including many lower-case, numerals, punctuation marks. 104pp. 8⅛ × 11. 24695-7 Pa. $8.95

HOW TO DO BEADWORK, Mary White. Fundamental book on craft from simple projects to five-bead chains and woven works. 106 illustrations. 142pp. 5⅜ × 8. 20697-1 Pa. $4.95

THE BOOK OF WOOD CARVING, Charles Marshall Sayers. Finest book for beginners discusses fundamentals and offers 34 designs. "Absolutely first rate . . . well thought out and well executed."—E. J. Tangerman. 118pp. 7¾ × 10⅝. 23654-4 Pa. $5.95

ILLUSTRATED CATALOG OF CIVIL WAR MILITARY GOODS: Union Army Weapons, Insignia, Uniform Accessories, and Other Equipment, Schuyler, Hartley, and Graham. Rare, profusely illustrated 1846 catalog includes Union Army uniform and dress regulations, arms and ammunition, coats, insignia, flags, swords, rifles, etc. 226 illustrations. 160pp. 9 × 12. 24939-5 Pa. $10.95

WOMEN'S FASHIONS OF THE EARLY 1900s: An Unabridged Republication of "New York Fashions, 1909," National Cloak & Suit Co. Rare catalog of mail-order fashions documents women's and children's clothing styles shortly after the turn of the century. Captions offer full descriptions, prices. Invaluable resource for fashion, costume historians. Approximately 725 illustrations. 128pp. 8⅜ × 11¼. 27276-1 Pa. $11.95

THE 1912 AND 1915 GUSTAV STICKLEY FURNITURE CATALOGS, Gustav Stickley. With over 200 detailed illustrations and descriptions, these two catalogs are essential reading and reference materials and identification guides for Stickley furniture. Captions cite materials, dimensions and prices. 112pp. 6½ × 9¼. 26676-1 Pa. $9.95

EARLY AMERICAN LOCOMOTIVES, John H. White, Jr. Finest locomotive engravings from early 19th century: historical (1804–74), main-line (after 1870), special, foreign, etc. 147 plates. 142pp. 11⅜ × 8¼. 22772-3 Pa. $10.95

THE TALL SHIPS OF TODAY IN PHOTOGRAPHS, Frank O. Braynard. Lavishly illustrated tribute to nearly 100 majestic contemporary sailing vessels: Amerigo Vespucci, Clearwater, Constitution, Eagle, Mayflower, Sea Cloud, Victory, many more. Authoritative captions provide statistics, background on each ship. 190 black-and-white photographs and illustrations. Introduction. 128pp. 8⅞ × 11¾. 27163-3 Pa. $13.95

EARLY NINETEENTH-CENTURY CRAFTS AND TRADES, Peter Stockham (ed.). Extremely rare 1807 volume describes to youngsters the crafts and trades of the day: brickmaker, weaver, dressmaker, bookbinder, ropemaker, saddler, many more. Quaint prose, charming illustrations for each craft. 20 black-and-white line illustrations. 192pp. 4⅝ × 6.　　　　　　　　　　　　　　　27293-1 Pa. $4.95

VICTORIAN FASHIONS AND COSTUMES FROM HARPER'S BAZAR, 1867–1898, Stella Blum (ed.). Day costumes, evening wear, sports clothes, shoes, hats, other accessories in over 1,000 detailed engravings. 320pp. 9⅜ × 12¼.
　　　　　　　　　　　　　　　　　　　　　　　　22990-4 Pa. $13.95

GUSTAV STICKLEY, THE CRAFTSMAN, Mary Ann Smith. Superb study surveys broad scope of Stickley's achievement, especially in architecture. Design philosophy, rise and fall of the Craftsman empire, descriptions and floor plans for many Craftsman houses, more. 86 black-and-white halftones. 31 line illustrations. Introduction. 208pp. 6½ × 9¼.　　　　　　　　　　　　27210-9 Pa. $9.95

THE LONG ISLAND RAIL ROAD IN EARLY PHOTOGRAPHS, Ron Ziel. Over 220 rare photos, informative text document origin (1844) and development of rail service on Long Island. Vintage views of early trains, locomotives, stations, passengers, crews, much more. Captions. 8⅞ × 11¾.　　　　26301-0 Pa. $13.95

THE BOOK OF OLD SHIPS: From Egyptian Galleys to Clipper Ships, Henry B. Culver. Superb, authoritative history of sailing vessels, with 80 magnificent line illustrations. Galley, bark, caravel, longship, whaler, many more. Detailed, informative text on each vessel by noted naval historian. Introduction. 256pp. 5⅜ × 8½.　　　　　　　　　　　　　　　　　　　　27332-6 Pa. $6.95

TEN BOOKS ON ARCHITECTURE, Vitruvius. The most important book ever written on architecture. Early Roman aesthetics, technology, classical orders, site selection, all other aspects. Morgan translation. 331pp. 5⅜ × 8½. 20645-9 Pa. $8.95

THE HUMAN FIGURE IN MOTION, Eadweard Muybridge. More than 4,500 stopped-action photos, in action series, showing undraped men, women, children jumping, lying down, throwing, sitting, wrestling, carrying, etc. 390pp. 7⅞ × 10⅝.
　　　　　　　　　　　　　　　　　　　　　　20204-6 Clothbd. $24.95

TREES OF THE EASTERN AND CENTRAL UNITED STATES AND CANADA, William M. Harlow. Best one-volume guide to 140 trees. Full descriptions, woodlore, range, etc. Over 600 illustrations. Handy size. 288pp. 4½ × 6⅜.
　　　　　　　　　　　　　　　　　　　　　　　　20395-6 Pa. $5.95

SONGS OF WESTERN BIRDS, Dr. Donald J. Borror. Complete song and call repertoire of 60 western species, including flycatchers, juncoes, cactus wrens, many more—includes fully illustrated booklet.　　Cassette and manual 99913-0 $8.95

GROWING AND USING HERBS AND SPICES, Milo Miloradovich. Versatile handbook provides all the information needed for cultivation and use of all the herbs and spices available in North America. 4 illustrations. Index. Glossary. 236pp. 5⅜ × 8½.　　　　　　　　　　　　　　　　25058-X Pa. $6.95

BIG BOOK OF MAZES AND LABYRINTHS, Walter Shepherd. 50 mazes and labyrinths in all—classical, solid, ripple, and more—in one great volume. Perfect inexpensive puzzler for clever youngsters. Full solutions. 112pp. 8⅛ × 11.
　　　　　　　　　　　　　　　　　　　　　　　　22951-3 Pa. $4.95

PIANO TUNING, J. Cree Fischer. Clearest, best book for beginner, amateur. Simple repairs, raising dropped notes, tuning by easy method of flattened fifths. No previous skills needed. 4 illustrations. 201pp. 5⅜ × 8½. 23267-0 Pa. $5.95

A SOURCE BOOK IN THEATRICAL HISTORY, A. M. Nagler. Contemporary observers on acting, directing, make-up, costuming, stage props, machinery, scene design, from Ancient Greece to Chekhov. 611pp. 5⅜ × 8½. 20515-0 Pa. $11.95

THE COMPLETE NONSENSE OF EDWARD LEAR, Edward Lear. All nonsense limericks, zany alphabets, Owl and Pussycat, songs, nonsense botany, etc., illustrated by Lear. Total of 320pp. 5⅜ × 8½. (USO) 20167-8 Pa. $6.95

VICTORIAN PARLOUR POETRY: An Annotated Anthology, Michael R. Turner. 117 gems by Longfellow, Tennyson, Browning, many lesser-known poets. "The Village Blacksmith," "Curfew Must Not Ring Tonight," "Only a Baby Small," dozens more, often difficult to find elsewhere. Index of poets, titles, first lines. xxiii + 325pp. 5⅜ × 8¼. 27044-0 Pa. $8.95

DUBLINERS, James Joyce. Fifteen stories offer vivid, tightly focused observations of the lives of Dublin's poorer classes. At least one, "The Dead," is considered a masterpiece. Reprinted complete and unabridged from standard edition. 160pp. 5³⁄₁₆ × 8¼. 26870-5 Pa. $1.00

THE HAUNTED MONASTERY and THE CHINESE MAZE MURDERS, Robert van Gulik. Two full novels by van Gulik, set in 7th-century China, continue adventures of Judge Dee and his companions. An evil Taoist monastery, seemingly supernatural events; overgrown topiary maze hides strange crimes. 27 illustrations. 328pp. 5⅜ × 8½. 23502-5 Pa. $7.95

THE BOOK OF THE SACRED MAGIC OF ABRAMELIN THE MAGE, translated by S. MacGregor Mathers. Medieval manuscript of ceremonial magic. Basic document in Aleister Crowley, Golden Dawn groups. 268pp. 5⅜ × 8½. 23211-5 Pa. $8.95

NEW RUSSIAN-ENGLISH AND ENGLISH-RUSSIAN DICTIONARY, M. A. O'Brien. This is a remarkably handy Russian dictionary, containing a surprising amount of information, including over 70,000 entries. 366pp. 4½ × 6⅛. 20208-9 Pa. $9.95

HISTORIC HOMES OF THE AMERICAN PRESIDENTS, Second, Revised Edition, Irvin Haas. A traveler's guide to American Presidential homes, most open to the public, depicting and describing homes occupied by every American President from George Washington to George Bush. With visiting hours, admission charges, travel routes. 175 photographs. Index. 160pp. 8¼ × 11. 26751-2 Pa. $10.95

NEW YORK IN THE FORTIES, Andreas Feininger. 162 brilliant photographs by the well-known photographer, formerly with *Life* magazine. Commuters, shoppers, Times Square at night, much else from city at its peak. Captions by John von Hartz. 181pp. 9¼ × 10¾. 23585-8 Pa. $12.95

INDIAN SIGN LANGUAGE, William Tomkins. Over 525 signs developed by Sioux and other tribes. Written instructions and diagrams. Also 290 pictographs. 111pp. 6⅛ × 9¼. 22029-X Pa. $3.50

THE INFLUENCE OF SEA POWER UPON HISTORY, 1660–1783, A. T. Mahan. Influential classic of naval history and tactics still used as text in war colleges. First paperback edition. 4 maps. 24 battle plans. 640pp. 5⅜ × 8½.
25509-3 Pa. $12.95

THE STORY OF THE TITANIC AS TOLD BY ITS SURVIVORS, Jack Winocour (ed.). What it was really like. Panic, despair, shocking inefficiency, and a little heroism. More thrilling than any fictional account. 26 illustrations. 320pp. 5⅜ × 8½.
20610-6 Pa. $8.95

FAIRY AND FOLK TALES OF THE IRISH PEASANTRY, William Butler Yeats (ed.). Treasury of 64 tales from the twilight world of Celtic myth and legend: "The Soul Cages," "The Kildare Pooka," "King O'Toole and his Goose," many more. Introduction and Notes by W. B. Yeats. 352pp. 5⅜ × 8½.
26941-8 Pa. $8.95

BUDDHIST MAHAYANA TEXTS, E. B. Cowell and Others (eds.). Superb, accurate translations of basic documents in Mahayana Buddhism, highly important in history of religions. The Buddha-karita of Asvaghosha, Larger Sukhavativyuha, more. 448pp. 5⅜ × 8½. ,
25552-2 Pa. $9.95

ONE TWO THREE . . . INFINITY: Facts and Speculations of Science, George Gamow. Great physicist's fascinating, readable overview of contemporary science: number theory, relativity, fourth dimension, entropy, genes, atomic structure, much more. 128 illustrations. Index. 352pp. 5⅜ × 8½.
25664-2 Pa. $8.95

ENGINEERING IN HISTORY, Richard Shelton Kirby, et al. Broad, nontechnical survey of history's major technological advances: birth of Greek science, industrial revolution, electricity and applied science, 20th-century automation, much more. 181 illustrations. ". . . excellent . . ."—Isis. Bibliography. vii + 530pp. 5⅜ × 8¼.
26412-2 Pa. $14.95

Prices subject to change without notice.

Available at your book dealer or write for free catalog to Dept. GI, Dover Publications, Inc., 31 East 2nd St., Mineola, N.Y. 11501. Dover publishes more than 500 books each year on science, elementary and advanced mathematics, biology, music, art, literary history, social sciences and other areas.